Sober Stick Figure

Sober Stick Figure

A MEMOIR   AMBER TOZER

RUNNING PRESS
PHILADELPHIA · LONDON

Published by Running Press,
A Member of the Perseus Books Group

Printed in China

Books published by Running Press are available at special discounts for bulk purchases in the United States by corporations, institutions, and other organizations. For more information, please contact the Special Markets Department at the Perseus Books Group, 2300 Chestnut Street, Suite 200, Philadelphia, PA 19103, or call (800) 810-4145, ext. 5000, or e-mail special.markets@perseusbooks.com.

Some names and identifying details have been changed
to protect the privacy of individuals.

ISBN 978-0-7624-5972-8

Library of Congress Control Number: 2015958287

E-book ISBN 978-0-7624-5974-2

9   8   7   6   5   4   3   2   1
Digit on the right indicates the number of this printing

Design by Joshua McDonnell
Edited by Jennifer Kasius
Typography: Brandon & Adobe Caslon
Front Cover Typography: © Thinkstock: iralu

Running Press Book Publishers
2300 Chestnut Street
Philadelphia, PA 19103-4371

Visit us on the web!
www.runningpress.com

This is a dark and funny story about alcoholism.

I hope it helps anyone who needs it.

For Grandma Babe

Chapter One

The first time I ever tasted alcohol was at my grandma Babe's house. I was seven years old. My uncle Woody let me take a swig of his beer, and I thought it tasted like sour pee. I knew what pee tasted like because I was a fucked-up kid. He also let me take a drag of his cigarette. Score! I felt like I was going to experience what men and loose women experienced in the movies, *extreme coolness*. As I took a big-ass toke off that cancer stick and my lungs filled with smoky chemicals it felt like my guts had just been set aflame. It felt horrible, like the most uncool thing I had ever done. I took another swig of beer then coughed so hard I almost threw up. Luckily, only long strings of saliva poured down my chin. My uncle smiled and said, "See. It's bad. You shouldn't drink and smoke." Then he took another puff.

My family said that Uncle Woody was an "alcoholic." They also said my dad and Grandpa Mac were "alcoholics." I could feel it in my bones that it was a very bad thing because when they said the word *alcoholic* their tone slipped into sadness. I intuitively knew that it was bad, but at the same time drinking alcohol was just something everyone did. I felt like I was hearing, "Alcohol is very bad, but everyone loves it and drinks it all of the time."

I probably thought this way because my parents owned a bar-restaurant called the Do Drop Inn, a local hot spot in my hometown of Pueblo, a midsize lower-middle-class city in the foothills of Colorado. Do Drop Inn, or better known as "the Do Drop," served pizza, burgers, and booze, and like all classic dive joints, had a dart board and a pool table. Me, my older brother Adam, and younger sister Autumn, were always around men who sat on stools with their elbows on the bar drinking one drink after another. They seemed fine. In fact, they made drinking alcohol look like a great idea. They were always laughing and smiling and when their favorite song came on the juke box they'd get up and dance. I loved walking in there with my family. Those boozy boys would pick me and Autumn up and say, "Hey, kiddos!" then toss us in the air. There is nothing more fun than being tossed in the air by a drunk when you're a kid. In that moment you feel both carefree and full of life.

I was happy my parents owned the bar; it was one of the coolest places in town. There's not much to do in Pueblo except breed and drink, so that's what everyone does. If you're not making babies, you're boozin'—sometimes people did these two things at the same time.

Mom's pizza recipe was a smash hit, and Do Drop became the number-one pizza place in town. Business was good, but I could tell something was wrong at home. My dad turned out to be a very sad and angry and depressed man. I had to take care of Autumn when my mom was at work because he wouldn't come out of his bedroom. I don't know if he was drinking in there or not because he kept the door closed. He slipped into a very dark depression that lasted years, and no one ever talked about it. I hated the silence.

Mom ended up divorcing him. She said the last straw was when he started hitting me and Adam with a cutting board. When my mom said we were moving out, I pretended to be sad because that's how kids acted in after-school specials when their parents got a divorce, but I was thrilled. I could not wait to get away. I hated him. Of course Mom got custody of us, and the cool thing was, my dad didn't want the Do Drop. He said if Mom gave him a lot of money she could have it.

So, she worked full-time at the gas station my aunt Sabrina owned until she made enough money to buy him out. Here she was, a newly single mom with full-time custody of three kids, going through a divorce, and working as a cashier at a gas station. I wondered what she was thinking, because you never knew, she was just always working toward a solution without emotion. I felt okay with everything because she seemed okay. I loved that she worked at a gas station because sometimes I'd go with her early in the morning before school and she would give me a day-old donut. Score.

My mom was a rock. She was a working warrior, doing whatever it took to maintain a stable life for us. I felt safe around her, but at the same time there was this hardness to her. Her style of lovin' was very tough, and she had no tolerance for feelings. I guess you can't be a softy when you have kids to feed and a fucked-up ex-husband. If she sat around and focused on her feelings she would have gone nuts. I believe my mom intuitively knew what to focus on to make things better, but what she didn't know is that we aren't all like that. I never, ever saw her feel sorry for herself, and that's how she wanted us to be.

My siblings and I handled the divorce pretty well. Adam was always focused on something like karate, bike riding, break dancing, or throwing Chinese stars at everyone. He did a good job keeping himself distracted. Autumn was real young, so I don't know if she knew what was happening, but she seemed okay. She was a mellow and sweet kid. I've always felt like an insane person no matter what was happening, so I guess I was feeling normal.

Okay, let me use these little stick-figure emoji bullet points to plow into this next portion of my life. After my parents got a divorce and my mom got the Do Drop, this stuff happened:

 My mom met and fell in love with a fireman named Mark. He had a big beer belly, but considered himself an athlete because he was good at sports in high school. I thought he was great because he at least came out of the bedroom. I was like, "This guy is great! He comes out of the bedroom to drink beer!" They got married and had my half sister, Rochelle. She was so cute.

 I was going through puberty and was full of suppressed rage and was mean to Autumn and Adam. I was also very horny. We all moved into a big house together "out in the country," and I loved my new school. I found an outlet for my pent-up rage and horniness—sports.

 Autumn, Adam, and I rarely saw my dad because he was still a mental mess.

 My mom was a workaholic and worked seven days a week at the Do Drop. Mark helped me with sports and took us camping and drank beer when he wasn't being a fireman.

I was content. I liked our new house, I was excelling in sports and school, and I loved my friends—but I had this other side of me, this nagging sense that I needed something else. Something was missing; it was like a lonely feeling, a pit in my stomach. I thought being a good kid would make me happy, but since it didn't, the dark side seemed very tempting.

Let's be
bad

Ok! I'm supposed to
be good but I
wanna be bad
so bad

This is why I wanted to try alcohol again. I wasn't a kid anymore taking baby sips of my uncle's beer; I was thirteen years old and ready to party my training-bra tits off. It was the summer of '89, and I was with my friend Tammy-Lou. She grew up in the country, so that's why her name is like that. She was a real tall girl with rich and cool parents. I loved her family. Tammy-Lou and I lived in the same neighborhood, went to school together, played sports together, and my stepdad was friends with her dad. I liked her because she was so much fun and laughed a lot. And if you did something stupid, she'd get a kick out of it and even encourage it. A perfect friend to have—tall, fun, funny, rich, sporty—and she enabled stupidity.

I'm rich and I'll pay you
$20 to hit yourself in the
head with a hammer

K

One night, Tammy-Lou was staying the night at my house, and we made a plan to sneak out and meet some boys we went to school with, Jason and Peter. These were the days before cell phones, so our plans consisted of one phone call to a landline and a lot of faith.

Teenagers Before Cell Phones

Hi. Want to sneak out and party

Yes

Hope this works out

I don't know where and when we're meeting but I'm sure it'll be fine

My house was super easy to sneak out of, especially on the night Tammy-Lou stayed over because my parents weren't even home. Mark was working an overnight fireman shift, my mom was working late at the Do Drop, and I don't remember where my siblings were. Hopefully, I didn't leave my little sisters home alone. Anyway, we could have just walked out the door, but I made Tammy-Lou crawl out a small window.

Why didn't we use the door

Because we're edgy and dangerous

I loved the feeling of doing something my parents would not want me to do; it was an adrenaline rush. The nagging dark side of me that wanted to be bad was finally being fed and the wrongness felt right. Even though sneaking out would be a mild thing to "bad kids," it was a huge deal to me. When you're an overachieving three-sport athlete who spends a lot of time making your hair perfect, sneaking out feels like you're committing a felony.

As Tammy-Lou and I walked in the dark, down the dirt road that led to the tennis courts, we could see Peter and Jason standing by the net. They were both tall, thin, and blond. Jason was a troublemaker; he was always doing crazy shit and getting in trouble. I liked him because he didn't give a fuck and wasn't intimidated by authority figures, or at least that's what it seemed like. Peter, on the other hand, was a good kid. Sort of like me, but not as needy and way more kind. Jason and Peter were best friends, probably drawn to each other because they were opposites.

As Tammy-Lou and I got closer to the courts, I got another burst of adrenaline. The thoughts in my mind were very staccato. We. Are. Sneaking. Out. To. Meet. Boys. And. Drink. Alcohol. SO. BAD.

We reached the tennis court entrance and greeted the boys with our awkward pubescent ways of communicating, which I'm sure involved a few insults. Maybe Tammy-Lou and I said something like, "Hey, dummies." And the boys said something like, "Hey, fatties." But I don't remember what we said. All I remember is Jason pulling out a huge bottle of Jim Beam from the inside pocket of his jean jacket and drinking it straight from the bottle. I could not believe how much he did not give a fuck about shit.

Peter was next. Jason passed him the bottle, and we all just stared at him waiting for him to take a drink. It was the rawest form of peer pressure. Eyes on you, Peter. Whatchya gonna do? He put the bottle to his lips and took a big swig, no big deal. I was pretty sure these two boys had done this before.

Then it was Tammy-Lou's turn. I knew she would be able to handle it because she was so tall and athletic. She took a swig, scrunched up her face, yelled "UGH," and passed the bottle to me. I could not wait to taste this disgusting beverage. I took a big drink real fast, wanting to get it over with. It tasted like something the devil made, but I enjoyed the warm sting as it traveled down my throat into my belly.

We continued to pass the bottle and drink. After a few more swigs, I was officially drunk and experiencing the psychic transformation that alcohol provides. It was like I had just poured a solution to all my problems over my mind.

Am I good enough
Do people like me

Before Alcohol

I'm the mother fuckin'
best motherfuckers

Jim
Beam

After Alcohol

I felt like a superhero, like a very hyper, athletic, sexy, smart, courageous, teenage superhero. I ran around hurdling the net and climbing the fence. I didn't know if I was showing off or trying to get my friends to worry about me. I liked the idea of being so crazy people worried about me. Then, I thought maybe I should kiss one of the boys, but I had no idea how to flirt, how to communicate, and my way of connecting with people was impressing them. But on this night, I realized all that shit didn't matter.

Tammy-Lou, Peter, and Jason stood in a huddle talking or whatever they were doing. I didn't know and I didn't really care because I could not contain my energy. Jason was usually the one to act like a nutjob, but on this night, it was my turn. I finally saw him as my equal. Jason was nothing but another kid on the planet. I was just as crazy as he was, and I would no longer hold him on a pedestal for being a bad kid who didn't give a fuck. *I* was the bad kid who didn't give a fuck. It was an incredible transformation. The nerves I had just an hour before were briefly drowned out by the voice of Jim Beam. A voice that I felt like I had been waiting for all my life.

I was feeling incredible and thought I should probably drink as much as possible so I could get MORE of those incredible feelings. I guess feeling drunk wasn't enough; the darkness that lurked inside of me kept telling me I needed MORE. I went from experiencing my first drunkenness to experiencing my first blackout in less than a couple of hours.

All I know is that I was at the tennis courts trying to be crazier than Jason, and the next thing I know I'm in my basement with Tammy-Lou and my mom having somewhat of a normal conversation. Apparently we had rushed back to my house, making it just in time before she got home from work. She brought us some pizza and asked us why we had our coats on. We couldn't say, "Oh, because we just got back from binge drinking whiskey with some bad boys at the tennis court, and we didn't have time to take our coats off before you got here," so I said, "We're cold." Tammy-Lou chimed in, "Yeah, it's cold in here." And that was it. Mom was sort of like "Huh, okay" and walked away to get ready for bed. She didn't know we were drunk AND she gave us Do Drop pizza. DRUNKEN SUCCESS STORY!

Okay, it wasn't a total success. I woke up a few hours later and threw up Jim Beam, pizza, and all the happy feelings that I thought would last forever. I laid on the bathroom floor like they do in the movies, curled up in a very dramatic fetal position wondering what had happened the night before, knowing that a chunk of time was missing. Flashbacks of running around the tennis courts and talking to my mom flooded my mind and filled me with dread. I promised myself I would never, ever drink again.

I have a new understanding of what hell is

Chapter Two

My first real addiction was attention and validation, so from the age of 15 to 18 I was focused on being the fucking best! These years are a blur of academic and athletic accolades and I rarely drank. When I was writing about all of this stuff I got bored. Here's what I looked liked when I originally wrote this chapter.

Honor Roll! Most Valuable Player! All-State! My bedroom wall was covered with awards. I'd look at them and daydream about the day I'd be someone really important.

Although I wasn't drinking during this phase of my life, it doesn't mean that I was free from alcoholism. I was surrounded by it and could not get away. I was like a pile of shit, and it was a fly. Let me see if I can draw that.

My dad was drinking, my stepdad Mark was drinking, my uncle Woody was drinking, and Grandpa Mac ended up dying of cirrhosis of the liver. Alcoholism was everywhere. It was the root of the dysfunction, but I never felt "too close" to it. It wasn't an obvious problem in my life. I rarely saw my dad, I didn't know my grandpa that well, and Mark and my uncle Woody were fun drunks. They came to life when they drank. They made jokes; they laughed and smiled more. It never occurred to me that it was genetic, and I was clueless that I was at risk of being an alcoholic. And I thought maybe drinking too much was a "guy" thing because all the women in my family were solid.

I THOUGHT MY GENDER WAS THE SUPERIOR ONE

Boy = Potential Alcoholic   Girls = Smarter than Boys

I never really registered how bad drinking was until the summer before my senior year. My cute little five-year-old sister Rochelle was riding with her best friend Chelsea and her family when they were hit head-on by a drunk driver who was going the wrong way on a major highway. Rochelle's best friend Chelsea died on the side of the road. She was six years old. Chelsea's loving and kind dad was crushed by the steering wheel and died instantly. Jennifer, Chelsea's older sister, made it out okay, and her mom, Linda, was stuck between the front and back seat and they had to use the jaws of life to remove her from the car—she survived. Lucky for the drunk driver, he died instantly. He escaped never knowing the horror he caused—the deaths, the pain, the broken bodies, and the broken hearts.

Drunk ↓

Shattered Lives ↓

Rochelle was hanging on for dear life and was flown on a flight-for-life helicopter to the hospital. She was in a coma with a concussion, a broken neck, and a lacerated spleen. The entire family rushed to the hospital to be with her. My mom was in tough-love mode, she was like, "Don't cry in front of her! She needs us to be strong!" We weren't allowed to be sad in front of Rochelle. We were all either in shock, weeping in the waiting room, or trying to stay busy by taking care of each other. The entire town sent flowers and food and prayers.

I couldn't process any emotion. I think we were all going insane, pacing and waiting and wondering if she was going to make it. Thank God she woke up and recovered like a champion-warrior, superhero baby girl.

Hospital Room

This accident shook our entire family to the core, and I vowed to never drink and drive. My senior year I was nominated for homecoming queen and my speech was about drinking and driving. I urged everyone to not do it, and I promised I wouldn't. I didn't win; a girl who joked about her dad's farts won.

Even though I wasn't homecoming queen and my sister almost died and the men in my family were drunks, I thought high school was a great experience. I was too wrapped up in my greatness to notice anything was wrong. I was on the honor roll all four years, racked up eleven varsity letters, a shit load of athletic awards, and a basketball scholarship. I worked my ass off and took all these accomplishments very seriously, and when it was time to finally graduate, I made the decision to drink as much alcohol as my body and mind would allow. I needed some relief. The pressure of being all I could be in high school really made me a high-strung asshole, and I needed a drink.

The night before graduation, my friend Bobby had a big party in the garage behind his house and it was so fun. There was a keg, random bottles of hard liquor, and weed everywhere. A bunch of football players, cowboys, cheerleaders, pot heads, and intellectuals were there. The best part about our senior class was the cliques clicked with each other, diversifying our parties. Cowboys would pour shots for the stoners; intellectuals told jokes to the jocks. It was such a fun-loving group of kids, and the alcohol helped us love each other even more.

We are all one

I decided to drink beer that night because I thought maybe it wouldn't make me throw up like Jim Beam did. I kept track of how many beers I drank. I wrote tally marks on my hand and ran around showing everyone, "Look, I've had seven cups of beer!" I think I got up to around eleven or twelve cups before I passed out in Bobby's pickup truck. It was a comfortable place to sleep until Bobby started banging on the driver's side window the next morning yelling at me because I got mud all over his seat and he said I peed in his mom's greenhouse.

During the graduation ceremony, I was so hungover and panicky. I didn't like seeing the friends I was with the night before because we were sober and awkward. I didn't remember everything that had happened and that made me nervous. I thought peeing in the greenhouse was funny, but I wondered what else I did and was thankful I did not take a shit in the greenhouse. As nice and open-minded as my friends were, they would have no problem nicknaming me "Tozer the Fertilizer."

It's the weirdest feeling to know just hours ago you were drunk and laughing and dancing and now you are nervous and shaky. It sucked because this was the day we had all been waiting for, and I was dry heaving and hiding behind sunglasses. I couldn't believe how unexcited I was about the entire ceremony. I think I did a good job pretending to be happy, but I just wanted it to be over.

After breakfast and getting a bunch of hugs and congratulations from friends and family, I felt better. My spirits were lifted, and my 17 year-old body recovered from the hangover. When my friends said what I thought were encouraging words, "Oh my God, you were so fucked-up last night. It was hilarious!", it made me happy. I forgot about those few hours of hell during the graduation ceremony and got excited about life again. High school was over! Holy shit! I was getting old!

I kept waiting to feel like an adult and wondered if I should I do my hair differently, read more books, or buy a purse. I didn't change much, I just partied a little bit more. I didn't drink often, but when I did, I drank A LOT. I remember one morning I woke up on the floor of my bedroom in a puddle of my pee.

When it came to drinking, I didn't know how to do it "right." I couldn't just have a couple, but I thought that was normal. And since I was only drinking once in a while, I was fine. I wasn't anything like my grandpa, my uncle, my dad, my stepdad, or that drunk driver who killed my sister's friend. I was just a kid doing what kids do. And I wasn't just any kid. I was special. I was a girl who did really well in high school and was going to college.

Chapter Three

The basketball scholarship I got was to a Division II school in Durango, Colorado, so that's where I went. I did not have a good time. Within the first month, I was overeating, and since I hated puking, I'd take laxatives and shit a lot. Then I was like, "This is disgusting" and got my pseudo eating disorder under control. I just felt trapped and needed some form of mutilation or stimulation. I couldn't party and socialize because there was no time. All I had time for was basketball practice, class, homework, and sleep, and the rest of the time I was crying.

September 1995

Sun	Mon	Tues	Wed	Thurs	Fri	Sat
cry	School B-ball cry	School B-ball cry	School B-ball cry	School B-ball cry	School B-ball cry	B-ball cry
cry	School B-ball cry	school B-ball cry	school B-ball cry	School B-ball cry	School B-ball cry	B-ball cry
cry	School B-ball cry	School B-ball cry	School B-ball cry	School B-ball cry	School B-ball cry	B-ball cry
cry	school B-ball cry	school B-ball cry	School B-ball cry	School B-ball cry	School B-ball cry	B-ball cry

We had a very intense conservative coach from the South who would yell, "MEANWHILE BACK AT THE RANCH," which meant, "You're slow and lazy and need to catch up." We were always in the gym lifting weights, so the freshman fifteen I gained was all muscle. I felt like I had lost control of my body because I didn't know what to do with my powerful muscles.

I couldn't quit basketball; I needed the scholarship money. I was like a basketball whore.

I lived in a dorm with the sweetest girl on the planet. I couldn't stand her, and I felt guilty about not liking her because she was so nice.

Thankfully, in the spring of my freshman year, an opportunity to move back home fell in my lap. The college in my hometown offered me a basketball scholarship! I could play basketball and go to school for free back home! I moved as soon as I was finished with the spring semester.

Adios, beautiful mountain town Durango. Hello, Pueblo, you sweet, little, lower-middle-class town in the foothills of Colorado. I was so happy. I loved Pueblo, and as much as my family drove me nuts, I missed them. I felt much more grounded being in that familiar environment, despite the fact that my mom had just divorced Mark because she said he drank too much and my biological father was on a downward mental illness and drinking spiral. It was okay. It felt normal, and I wanted to be there.

I didn't blame my mom for divorcing Mark. She said his boozin' was getting out of control, and she worried that he was drinking and driving. She couldn't deal with the thought of that after their daughter had been seconds away from death at the hands of a drunk driver. My mom's life was riddled with alcoholism, and she didn't even drink! Her dad was an alcoholic, my dad was an alcoholic, and now maybe Mark was one. She'd had it! She'd always say, "No more alcoholics!" She was very matter of fact about this divorce, no signs of sadness, no complaining about her situation—just a lot of action to move on.

My dad during this time—oh God, he just kept getting worse. I wasn't sure if he was drinking or if he had just lost his mind, but I couldn't be around him for more than an hour. He was full of negativity, and my stomach would fill up with acid when he was around. I blocked out all of this family crap. I had to focus on myself. I was moving back home. I had to switch schools and prepare for another year of college basketball. STRESSED!

That summer I found some relief working at the Do Drop as a waitress. It was such a fun place to work. My mom had moved the business to a bigger location, so it felt more like a restaurant than a bar, but people were always drinking there. Our customers were a good mix of families, young people, and your hard-core drunks. We'd occasionally have to ask people to leave or cut them off; that's how it was at every bar in town. People in Pueblo love to party, man.

I became good friends with another waitress there, Lisa. She was from Chicago. I loved that she was from out of town, and I loved the way she talked. She was super quick, had a funny Chicago accent, and told the best stories. Her timing with jokes was incredible, and no one had ever made me laugh so hard in my life.

THE DO DROP INN

Ha Ha Ha!
Ha Ha Ha!

Beers on Tap

Me & Lisa

I had
too many

One day she was like, "I want to go on a road trip to Crater Lake, Oregon." I said, "I'll go with you." A few weeks later we were on a cross-country road trip on our way to Crater Lake, Oregon, in my 1990 extended cab Nissan pickup truck. It was 1997, and we used a real map to find our way.

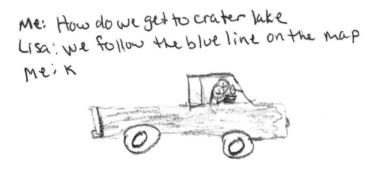

Me: How do we get to crater lake
Lisa: we follow the blue line on the map
Me: K

I was only nineteen but had a fake ID. Well, it was a real ID that I stole from a bitchy girl who forgot it at the Do Drop. I was her waitress, and she was so mean to me. After she paid her bill, I noticed she left her driver's license on the table. I could have easily ran and given it to her as she walked out to the parking lot, but I picked it up and looked at it. "Hmmm, brown hair, brown eyes, twenty-three years old. I could use this!" I put it in my pocket. Since she was such an asshole, I didn't feel guilty about stealing it. I tried it out at a bar, and I was sort of offended when it worked because I thought she was ugly.

Door Man: OK you can go in
me: Are you serious

Colorado Driver License
94 371 8431
DOB - 05-18-1974
Eyes Brown
Hair - Brown
Ugly Girl Ht: 5'3 Wt: 140
147 mean Ave
Pueblo, CO

BAR   LADIES NIGHT
Happy Hour
Buy 7 Get 1 Free

ugly ID

But thank God for that ugly girl ID, because I needed it to party on our road trip. We drove through Salt Lake City up to Oregon, doing bong hits and laughing our asses off the entire way.

Crater Lake was incredible; it's a volcano that collapsed and filled up with rain. It had the bluest water I had ever seen, and it was only 30 degrees. Some boys were cliff jumping into it, and Lisa and I decided that we should do it too. When I hit the water, I went under a few feet, then popped back up with my mouth open and screaming so loud. It was one of the moments I knew I'd always remember. It was terrifying and exhilarating, and I was just so damn happy to be alive. Euphoria took over, and I made a mental note to take more risks in the future. Jumping in Crater Lake sparked my first moment of clarity, and I wanted to hold on to that feeling. I assumed that, in order to feel euphoric, I was going to have to keep doing crazy things that scared me.

We drove down the Pacific Coast to San Francisco and stayed with one of Lisa's friends who was a scientist with a real fancy job. The scientist friend had an eccentric neighbor who invited us over. She told us about an S&M club and said we should go. She even gave us sexy, black leather outfits to borrow. Lisa wore a skimpy shirt that landed around her upper thighs so it was good enough to double as a short skirt, and I had on thigh-high, black leather boots and a black leather top that was too big for me.

The S&M club was insane. There were people dry humping everywhere and hanging off contraptions from the ceiling, and there was a softcore-porn sex show happening on a big stage. One guy onstage poured water down his back. Then a lady touched his lower back with an electrical stun-gun thing, and blue shock waves traveled up the streams of water on his body. Lisa and I were like "Holy shit," and then we started pounding alcohol.

We tried to fit in, but it was pretty obvious we were white trash. These people were full of culture and sophistication and lots of experiences with hot sex. Lisa and I danced around, tried to meet people, and got real fuckin' sloshed. We drank Long Island Iced Teas because those have a lot of booze. There's not even any tea in them at all!

Long Island Iced Tea

Ingredients
Vodka
Gin
Rum
Tequila
Triplesec
Splash of Coke
NO TEA
Sadness
rage
false confidence
misguided horniness
regret

Directions
Dump it all in a glass and slam it and do dumb things and wake up and do your best to get through the day without crying

I loved the manufactured feeling alcohol gave me. It gave me bad ideas that I thought were 100 percent great, and the confidence to take action on them. It turned me into the same superhero I was at the tennis courts that night with Tammy-Lou. I loved myself and I didn't give a shit about what anyone thought. The feeling of not caring is what I loved the most. Alcohol shut down the negative voices in my head and replaced them with a twisted, positive voice that said, "You're amazing. Do something crazy, everyone will love it."

So, in this mindset, after the sex show I hopped up on that stage. There was a bar that ran across part of the stage that was about 8 feet above the ground. I jumped up and grabbed it and started doing pull-ups. I wanted to show off my ripped arms. As I was doing pull-ups, a guy walked by and I wrapped my legs around his head and would not let go. I thought I was being sexually aggressive, but he hated it and tried to break free from my tight thigh grip. His face was in my crotch, and I just kept squeezing his head so hard. Lisa was on the ground laughing, and I felt like I did at Crater Lake, so happy to be alive even though it was at the expense of some stranger's neck.

That trip changed my life. It made me want to explore the world. It inspired me to be more artsy and less jockey, and I also began to think that partying was a very, very good thing. I wanted to do it more. It was SO FUN. But I still had three years left of college basketball. UGH. I was hoping basketball at this new school would be better than it was in Durango. I pulled it together just in time for my sophomore year. I decided to major in business because I love thinking about different ways to make money.

Basketball was not better at this school. Of course the coaches turned out to be overbearing whack-attacks with Charlie Manson eyes. I came to the conclusion that college coaches never really reached their true athletic potential, and, therefore, project the success they wish they had on others, forcing them to be great at any cost.

The upside was I loved my teammates. We would party during school breaks and over the summer. I was pretty good about not drinking too much during the season, but when I did drink I drank like an obese pig. It was weird, even when I tried to have just a couple, I couldn't. If I had one, I had to have more—just like Mark and Uncle Woody and the guys at the Do Drop. I thought maybe when you drank you're supposed to drink a lot. I developed a mindset that told me the main purpose of drinking was to get FUCKED-UP. The only reason alcohol was invented was to lose your mind, make bad choices, and then have an easy way to justify your behavior.

I invented this so people can lose their Goddamned minds

Inventor of
Alcohol

One time, the entire team went dancing at the only club in town, Peppers. Thursday night was college night, and if you were eighteen you could get in. We drank Mad Dog in the parking lot, and once we were in the club, our main goal was to find older boys to buy us alcohol. I got so fucking wasted that night, and it felt incredible.

There was a dance contest, and I said, "Aw shit. It's on." It was one of those contests where you dance and show off your moves. A judge walks around and if he or she taps you on the shoulder, it means you're out. Well, some guy came around and tapped me on the shoulder and told me I was out. I thought, "Yeah, right." I ran off the dance floor and put on my friend's sweater and put my hair in a ponytail so I looked like a different person and went back out there and ended up winning! I went up to the DJ booth and gave a speech, even though that wasn't what you were supposed to do.

It was amazing, and I thought I was very special. Then we all went back to this girl Tina's apartment to crash. She was a shooting guard, and had the cutest nose ever. I was sleeping in her bed and had a dream about urinating in the Colorado Rockies. I woke up and walked to the corner of her bedroom, pulled down my pants, and peed in the corner. I thought I was in the mountains pissing like a pioneer. Tina was in the room on the phone with her boyfriend giving him a play by play of what was happening. I went back to bed like nothing happened.

Since Tina's boyfriend was a player on the boys' basketball team and had a big mouth; my nickname quickly became "squat." Everyone in the basketball community knew what I had done, and it was actually sort of funny because everyone got a kick out of my pee story. I wasn't that embarrassed—I sort of liked the attention. It was funny! I was such a funny girl! Partying so hard and peeing everywhere was endearing!

I just realized this is the third pee story I've told. Don't worry, there are more. Anyway, I had these short benders of pure drunken fun, but managed to keep my drinking under control. I spent the majority of my college years working hard at school and working even harder trying to keep my shit together. I felt like I was burning up on the inside, like I was going to explode. It was like there was another person living inside of me who didn't want what I had. Something that made me feel like I wasn't enough.

During my junior year, I ended up quitting basketball. I had to. I was done. The money was not worth it anymore. I just wanted to go to school, do some traveling, and figure out what I was going to do after college. It felt so weird walking away from something I used to care so much about, but it was a huge relief. I had no idea how good quitting could feel.

My senior year, I moved in with my grandma Babe and made school a priority, but I also started partying more than I ever had before. My drinking went from every few months to every weekend. Then, I started showing up drunk to night classes and one time a professor busted me. He pulled me outside into the hallway and told me that he knew I was drunk. He said he could smell it. I said, "Oh, I worked at my mom's restaurant today, and a customer spilled a beer on me." He looked at me sideways and let me go back to class. The thing about lying when you're drunk is, you believe the lie. Your denial is incredible. The second I came up with that lie I felt like he was an idiot for even questioning me. And you know how I got to class? I drove drunk. Yep, little miss "don't drink and drive because my sister almost died" was driving drunk to school.

Deep down I knew I was fucked-up for drinking and driving, but the excuses I came up with were so good I'd talk myself out of feeling bad about it. I became a master at this. Anytime I did something crazy when I was drunk, I was able to convince myself that it was okay. And no matter how obvious my occasional insanity was, I truly felt like I was fine. Sure, I liked to party, but when I was at home with my grandma, my life was really quiet, calm, and peaceful.

I was working and going to school and ended up graduating with a BSBA in Business Administration. I didn't even know what that meant. I was like, "Um. Okay. Guess I'm a businesswoman now. Location. Location. Location."—that's the only thing I remembered about marketing class.

I had been listening to Tony Robbins's *Personal Power* CDs and convinced myself that I should move to New York City. I was going to do it. I told Lisa, my family, and all of my coworkers at the Do Drop. I'm not sure if they believed me or not. I didn't care. I was moving there by myself because I was in a blackout of positive thinking.

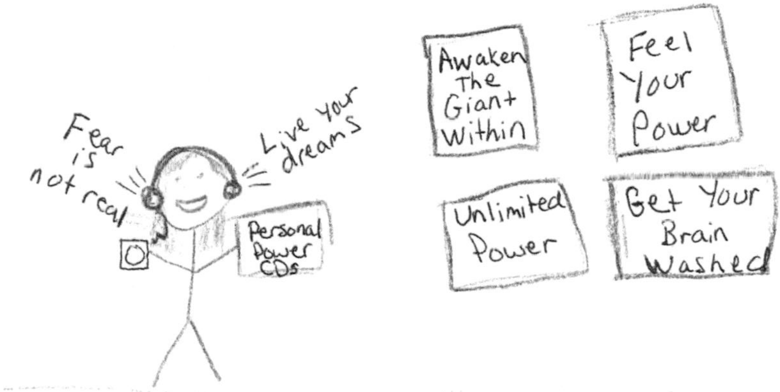

Fear is not real

Live your dreams

Personal Power CDs

Awaken The Giant Within

Feel Your Power

Unlimited Power

Get Your Brain Washed

I had been to NYC once, for a few days with my friend Danielle, a hilarious girl who worked at the Do Drop. She was always like, "Oh my God! What the fuck?" over everything, even if ice melted or something obvious and normal happened. She'd be so animated about it. She was the perfect friend to go to New York with, because both of us were always screaming DID YOU SEE THAT and THAT GUY WAS SUCH A WEIRDO and ARE WE GONNA DIE? Just like San Francisco, there was something about this city that made me feel like I didn't know anything about life. I wanted to know more about everything—art, food, culture, sex—and I wanted to know how to get a big-city attitude.

Danielle and I only spent a few days there. We didn't even take the subway because it was too overwhelming for us, but getting wasted and hanging out with strangers felt safe. I made out with an Italian boy in the back of a cab and then never talked to him again. Danielle and I went rollerblading in Central Park, got swindled in Chinatown, and then we met a nice Indian man at a bar. He let us stay at his apartment in Midtown for free! He didn't even do anything perverted, and I took his kindness as a sign to move there.

When I was planning my move, I didn't have many options. My plan was to save up money over the summer, buy a one-way ticket, and go. I kept listening to Tony and writing, "I will find an apartment and a job in New York and live my dreams." I had to keep telling myself why I was doing this, otherwise I'd chicken out.

I had to organize the reasons in my head, and it basically came down to understanding that if I stayed in Pueblo I'd have limited options. I'd most likely end up working for my mom at the Do Drop, which offered a lot of security. But I didn't want security, I wanted opportunities and adventures. I worked for my mom for a few years; I was over it. I didn't want to stay and work there and look back on my youth and wonder what else I could have done. I wanted to maybe be an actress or a successful businesswoman or get famous because famous people are loved and have great skin and swimming pools. I needed a big city, but first I was going to save up some money and party my fucking ass off with my friends in Pueblo.

Lisa and I knew this was going to be our last summer together and decided to do something crazy. We needed one last life-changing journey and decided to drive from Pueblo to Key West because it was only 2,200 miles away. I hope you're not like, "OH NO, NOT ANOTHER ROAD-TRIP STORY." Just keep reading, because what else are you gonna do? Stalk your ex on social media and get sad?

This road trip could not be any more different from the Crater Lake and S&M club trip. Lisa and I were older, smarter, college graduates with big plans for our future, so our partying was a celebration of life and when we smoked pot it was like a religious experience. And we almost died once and were always one step away from being thrown in jail. You might begin to ask yourself, is this book a thriller or a memoir?

This is you on the edge of your seat

I'll never forget the day we left for this trip. It was May 3, 1999, and we were hauling ass east in my good ol' pickup truck, the same truck that got us to Crater Lake and San Fran. We drove all day long, and just as the sun was setting, we crossed the border of Oklahoma and thought it was a good time to start smoking the killer weed Adam had given us.

We were tokin', smokin', and laughin', and I felt so free and was thinking about the future. I thought about how great my life was going to be. I loved smoking pot in the right environment. Sometimes it made me paranoid, but sometimes it made me feel like I was one with life. We were driving fast and listening to Will Smith's *Willennium* album, and we got mad at him. We said, "He needs to get over himself. Who names an entire millennium after themselves?" We were judging his attitude and acting out conversations we would have with him.

All of a sudden, it got windy. Like, really, really windy. It felt like the hand of an angry god was pushing my truck off the road, and I didn't even believe in any gods. I was scared, but I just thought I was paranoid because I was so stoned. Lisa was like, "Dude. You are holding on to that steering wheel so tight. Your arms are bulging out." I said, "It's fucking windy out there!" The sky turned black and lightning storms started to dance in the sky.

Just as we hit Oklahoma City, we saw trash and debris everywhere. We just thought the town was dirty, but then emergency vehicles flew past us, ambulances, cop cars, security vehicles, and we could not figure out what was going on. In our stoned state of mind Lisa said, "I think something serious happened," and I said, "Yeah, maybe we should turn on the radio." We turned off Will Smith and turned on local stations with DJs screaming, "This is the biggest tornado storm we've had in over 60 years. An F4 just ripped through Oklahoma City, and there are many more in the surrounding areas. Take cover." I thought about how high we were and how we didn't even know we were driving straight into a tornado storm. My brother always had the best weed.

We spent the next few hours hovered in a shower stall at a truck stop taking cover with strangers and a little boy who threw up everywhere. I noticed he had eaten cereal and thought his parents were either cool for letting him have cereal for dinner, or neglectful because he hadn't eaten since breakfast time. We were just sitting there waiting for a tornado to hit us. It didn't. It missed us by a half mile, and we all survived. Lisa and I called our moms to tell them what happened. They said they had been talking to each other and wondering if we were alive because they had been watching the news. We were fine, just exhausted and in shock.

We weren't able to laugh about it until we got to Florida. My aunt Pam lived in Orlando, so we stopped and stayed with her for a few days. We were so smelly and disgusting, and she washed our clothes. My uncle Jim helped us fix the truck window that broke during the tornado. My cousins Shannon and Kim thought we were crazy, but I think they liked listening to our stories.

They were real clean and proper, so we made sure to get stoned in the upstairs bathroom so no one would know. We blew the smoke into the toilet and flushed it. One night, we got stoned and were standing at the top of the stairs, getting ready to go down to the kitchen to get a snack. My aunt's house was spotless. The carpet was soft and smooth, and my feet slipped out from under me like a cartoon character who just stepped on a banana peel. My feet were air-born and my body turned stiff. I was completely straight with my hands down by my sides. I flew down the stairs like a bobsled and popped back up at the bottom. Lisa was at the top of the stairs, losing her mind in a fit of giggles. I was in physical pain from laughing so hard. I loved that moment so much because the stakes were just as high as we were. If my aunt busted us getting stoned in her house, she might tell my mom and I'd get in trouble. I felt so edgy.

The next night, we went to Pleasure Island, a strip of bars and nightclubs in Downtown Disney, a place where people could party at Disney World. My cousin Kim came with us, she was super straight-laced and was afraid of sinning. We inspired her to sin and encouraged her to get wasted.

We ended up at a dance club, and a girl started dancing with me. She was rubbing up on me all sexy, and I went with it. I thought it was funny. We were grinding like stupid, drunk white girls do, and a big bro–type guy tapped me on the shoulder and said, "That's my girlfriend, you dyke." I was so mad. I was like, "Well, maybe you're not giving her what she needs" and then he pushed me! Then he pushed his girlfriend! Lisa took a swing at him and missed. It was like a scene from an eighties movie where sweaty, skinny white boys with cigarettes dangling from their mouths get into a bar fight, then run away when the cops get there.

The doorman broke up the fight, and we all got kicked out. Kim was having a panic attack, and we had to call my aunt Pam to come and pick us up. We didn't want to leave without making it a true, hard parting experience, so while we were waiting for her to come and get us, Lisa and I peed in the parking lot.

Lisa and I were just your typical party girls—drinking, clubbing, getting in fights with dumb men. But being around my conservative family made it seem as if we were on our way to hell, and if they weren't careful we'd bring them with us. When you're a drunk surrounded by other drunks, you're normal. When you're a drunk surround by conservatives, you're nothin' but trouble.

I liked that they thought we were nuts and out of control. I loved that we got in trouble and that we were drunk and stoned all of the time. Maybe it was because I was still blowing off steam from taking sports and school so seriously, but my appetite for partying was getting bigger. I loved it. Drinking was becoming a part of my identity, and I had completely let go of my college-athlete persona.

Lisa and I continued on our journey toward the Florida Keys. We stopped in Key Largo and met a guy in a hotel lobby and ended up sharing a room with him to save money. We weren't scared; he seemed normal and nice. He was there for a bartending convention and told us we should go. We did. It was like an MTV beach party but with uglier people. There were a lot of liquor distributors there, giving away free booze on the beach. We told them that we were bartenders in Colorado at the Do Drop Inn and got unlimited free booze. We drank that free alcohol like a marathon runner would drink water after crossing the finish line in the Sahara. I made out with an older man with halitosis, and Lisa stripped down to her to her underwear and jumped in the ocean.

I don't remember what else happened, but I do remember Lisa drunk driving us back to our hotel and getting lost. We were in a really deep conversation, you know those conversations you get into when you're drunk and stoned and you're talking about the meaning of life and you figure it out together. We finally found our hotel and the stranger we shared the room with didn't even murder us. We were so lucky.

On our way back to Colorado, we were exhausted but managed to stop in New Orleans and Austin and got very fucking drunk in both cities. When we made it back to Pueblo, we told everyone our crazy stories and got on with our lives. Lisa had a boyfriend and they were getting serious, and I was obsessed with my move to New York. I was working at the Do Drop during the day and bartending at a dance club in Pueblo West at night. I wanted to save up at least five thousand dollars for the big move. I saved money by living with Grandma Babe and eating for free at the Do Drop. I'd stash all of my tips in a big bucket in my bedroom.

When I wasn't working or drinking, I was at the school library using the Internet. I'd research New York City and try to find an apartment. There weren't that many websites for apartment rentals back in 1999. It seemed like it was going to be impossible, but I met one guy online who seemed nice and normal. His name was Jeff. He was renting a room in Queens. He had to rent it out right away, so he gave the room to someone else. But we began a friendly e-mail relationship and planned to meet up when I got to New York.

To Do List

- ☑ Get drunk in New Orleans
- ☑ Get drunk in Austin
- ☑ Sleep at Grandma Babe's
- ☑ Work at Do Drop + Dance Club
- ☑ Email Strangers on the Internet
- ☐ Save $5,000
- ☑ Become very delusional

It was weird talking to my family and friends about moving. I don't think they could comprehend or understand why I was doing it. A few people were like, "Pssshhh. You're moving to New York? Yeah right" or "You'll only last a day out there." Some people were supportive and said stuff like, "Good for you. You only live once."

I loved talking to my aunt Sabrina because she was positive and encouraging and she said she worried that I was going by myself, but to go for it. She'd say, "Live your dreams, girl!" I also loved talking to Hoss, the manager of the Do Drop. He had worked for my mom ever since I could remember and had become like a psuedo father figure. He truly cared about me and my siblings. He'd offer guidance and support, and my family loved him. He was from Iran and couldn't go back there because they would kill him. He had an accent that made whatever he said sort of funny, especially when he messed up catchphrases or tried to speak in American slang.

We'd sit down and have heart to hearts, and sometimes I'd cry when I talked to him. I don't know why. I think maybe because I didn't have a lot of "big picture" conversations with anyone (besides Lisa when we were wasted). When I talked to Hoss about leaving my family and trying new things, I would weep because he was so sweet about it. He said he believed in me, and I could always go back to Do Drop if I wanted.

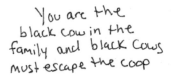

You are the black cow in the family and black Cows must escape the coop

It's black sheep and chickens fly the coop but thanks for your support

I drank like a pig all summer. I started fantasizing about drinking during the day because it made me feel good just knowing that I'd be buzzed soon. Simply thinking about getting drunk was very comforting to me. Partying was slowly becoming one of my main priorities, and I'd seek out ways to drink, even sneaky ways. Sometimes I'd slip some vodka in my soda at work or have drinks BEFORE I went out drinking. When I was sneaky about it, I knew it was a little "off," but being drunk made me feel so incredible, I didn't care. And everyone I knew drank a lot, so I fit in. I was just like everyone else.

The people who worked at the Do Drop were my favorite party pals. There is nothing like getting tanked after a long and busy waitressing shift. Danielle, Lisa, a few other waitresses, and some of the cooks would meet at Eiler's, a dive bar down the street from the Do Drop. Lisa and I would dance on the bar and take off our bras and smack the bartender in the face with them. I would drink Colorado Bulldogs—they're White Russians with a splash of Coke. They tasted like tiny little milk shakes. I loved how hyper and confident I would get after I had five of them.

Occasionally, I'd party with my family. My aunt Jacque and uncle Bob were a blast to drink with; both of them were very funny. Jacque would tell a joke, and Bob would have a tagline for it, and then they'd both crack up at themselves. One time, they had a huge party at their house. Lisa and I showed up like we were doing everyone a favor for being there. My aunt Sabrina and uncle Sam brought over some moonshine and everyone got plastered. People were literally howling at the moon.

Lisa and I kept playing "Wannabe" by the Spice Girls over and over. Bob hated that song and said he was going to either shoot us or shoot himself because he hated that song. We were like, "Shoot yourself!" and then we'd play the song again. Then Jacque made us turn it off because she said Bob was seriously going to shoot us. We said okay because he had guns in the basement.

Then we found other ways to be obnoxious. The salsa dip plate was shaped like a sombrero. Lisa put it on her head, and it fell off and salsa spilled everywhere. I loved the nonsense. I loved laughing at something I would normally be worried about.

To be unapologetic and full of confidence felt incredible. It was like a spiritual experience. I spent so much time worrying about everything and trying to get people to like me. Not caring about anything made me feel like I was connected to some all-knowing being that made whatever choice I made feel like the right one. Alcohol had a powerful effect over me, and I was completely unaware of how much I needed it.

I'd drink with whoever would drink with me, even my mom. She didn't drink much, but her crew of fun-lovin', happy-hour-goin', middle-aged lady friends would throw 'em back a couple nights a week, and I'd meet up with them and let them buy me drinks. I liked drinking with older people because their conversations were different than the ones I had with my friends. They talked about mortgages and ex-husbands and if they said something a little edgy, they'd laugh real loud about it. I'd have a few with them, then go have a few more at another bar with friends, then after the bar closed we'd go to someone's house and drink more. It was the perfect party schedule. All I knew, or I guess didn't know, or pay attention to: If I had one, I had to have a lot. The second I got that warm fuzzy confident feeling, I craved more, and after I was already drunk and wobbly, I still craved more.

I don't think I spent much time with Autumn and Rochelle that summer. Autumn was a teenager, and Rochelle was in middle school, both too young to party. Sorry, little sisters! I should have been taking them to the movies or to the mall or something cool big sisters do, but I didn't because I only gravitated toward people and situations that involved alcohol.

That's why I loved hanging with Adam and his crew. They were a bit older than me and were always gave me booze and pot. They taught me that watching the Animal Channel when you're high is one of the funniest things you'll ever experience, because when turtles have sex they grunt like porn stars. Since I was open to experimenting with different ways to get high, I was thrilled when one of Adam's friends offered me mushrooms, which, I discovered, enhanced whatever mood I was in to the millionth degree. One time I took them and I could not stop crying; an other time I took them I could not stop dancing.

Every time I drank or did a drug, I could not believe how much it changed me. For the most part, I would just turn into this version of the person I wanted to be—wild, fun, crazy, funny, confident, and sexy. I was probably just obnoxious, but in my mind, I was the best. I began to not like the person I was when I was sober. When I was sober, I was sort of serious and cranky. I knew that if I just had a few drinks in me, I'd be more likable, or more importantly I'd FEEL more likable.

I don't remember what else happened that summer. I just remember working a lot, drinking a lot, and living with my sweet grandma Babe. She was hilarious and very nice to everyone, and I loved that she didn't tell me what to do or try to control me. She was always asking me questions about my life and telling me to take off my pants so she could wash them. Whenever she saw me drunk, all she'd do is wave her finger at me and shake her head like, "That stuff is bad news, kid." She had lost her husband to alcoholism, and her son (Uncle Woody) was following in his footsteps.

The summer was coming to an end. I bought a one-way ticket to NYC, put my notice in at the Do Drop and the dance club, and figured out what stuff to put in my two suitcases. I saved up six thousand dollars and thought I was so rich. I gave my grandma a care package and thanked her for letting me stay with her all summer. It had a book, some money, a white sweatshirt with an illustration of a teddy bear holding a balloon, and some chocolate. My family and friends threw a surprise going-away party for me at Eiler's, and I felt very, very loved and supported. We all drank like sailors on a sinking ship. After the bar closed down, a few of us ended up driving out to the Pueblo reservoir and sat by the lake and stared at the stars. I was ready to go.

OKAY, ARE YOU READY? HERE COMES MY BIG MOVE TO NEW YORK. IT WAS MY FIRST STEP TOWARD ROCK BOTTOM. IT WAS LIKE ONE OF THOSE STEPS YOU TAKE RIGHT INTO A PILE OF DOG SHIT, BUT YOU DON'T REALIZE IT UNTIL YOU GET HOME.

Chapter Five

My mom and some of her happy-hour gal pals flew out to NYC with me to drop me off, turning my big move into an opportunity to vacation in the Big A. I was a little annoyed by this because I pictured my arrival to NYC to be like something you'd see in the movies. Ya know—a young girl steps off a bus, sets her suitcases down, looks up at the skyscrapers with her big eyes, and takes a deep breath as she takes it all in. She jumps up real high and throws a victory fist in the air, then a taxi drives through a puddle and she's sprayed with dirty water—a sign this city is tough to live in, but she's gonna do it anyway. Instead, I was surrounded by a bunch of small-town, middle-aged women with hair-sprayed hairdos and way too much luggage screaming, "OH MY GOD. THERE ARE SO MANY PEOPLE HERE. WHERE DO WE GET A CAB? WHERE'S OUR HOTEL? MY FEET HURT."

Where's Times Square

It's in middle earth on your way to hell

Since I didn't have an apartment, or a job, or friends, or street-smarts, I think my mom was freaking out that I was actually doing this. I didn't know anything about this city! I didn't even know how to take the subway! It suddenly hit me that all I had was a bachelor's degree from an unknown university, some Tony Robbins positive thinking strategies, and an unclear dream of "making it big." I had to get city savvy, and I had to do it fast.

I stayed with the gaggle of cougars for a week in a hotel room and slept on a cot. While they went shopping and to Broadway shows, I scoured classified newspapers and started making phone calls and appointments for both job interviews and potential roommate situations. My mom went with me to look at apartments, and as tough as she was, I could tell she was on the brink of a mini nervous breakdown. The thought of me living in NYC was so extreme to her.

The last roommate I had was my grandma. We lived in a cozy three-bedroom house and kept an extra key in the mailbox for anyone who wanted to come in. Now I was looking for a home that would most likely be the size of a walk-in closet, decorated with rat traps and gates on the window. One of the places we looked at was in Hell's Kitchen. The guy renting the room was a very cool, older Rastafarian man with dreads who took us to the rooftop to show us the view of the city, it was great. We had a bird's-eye view of the Port Authority bus station and we got to see a mix of commuters, homeless people, and runaways hanging around the station. As the three of us looked out at the skyscrapers, my mom opened up to him and expressed her concern about me moving to the city alone. He said, "It's time to let her go, Mom," and she started crying. This was only the second time I'd ever seen my mom cry; the other time was when my grandpa died.

I was standing on a building in the biggest city in the world and the only thing I could see were my mother's tears

As my mom and I took the subway and went to different neighborhoods looking for a place for me to move into, my mind sort of went into shock. It felt way different than when Danielle and I took our trip to NYC. I think because I knew I'd be staying. My senses were on fire. I'd lived the majority of my life in very quiet neighborhoods, going to the same places, seeing the same people, having the same conversations. When I stood in the street and looked at the skyscrapers and all of the restaurants and all of the bars and bookstores and delis and shoe repair shops and designer clothing stores and theaters and apartment buildings and all of the people and traffic, I thought I might die from a heart attack. I'd calm myself down using Tony Robbins's techniques, ignoring the fear and staying focused on the goal—find a job and an apartment.

Hi I'm supposed to be fear

Death
Failure
Weakness
Emotional Torture

Hi FUCK OFF

I called Jeff, my e-mail pal, to let him know that I was in town. We met for a beer at an Irish pub in Midtown, and I was so relieved he looked normal and had on nice clothes and he seemed happy to meet me. He ordered a bottle of Bud, which I thought was weird. Shouldn't he be ordering something more fancy since he lived in NYC? I ordered a draft beer, one I had never heard of before. It was so good, thicker and tastier than the keg beer I used to drink in garages back home. I drank it real fast, then ordered a vodka cranberry because I wanted something stronger and healthier. I hoped Jeff was paying because these drinks were way more expensive than they were in Pueblo.

It felt good to be on my own away from my mom and her friends, drinking with a stranger I met on the Internet. Jeff ended up being a very nice guy, which meant I wasn't attracted to him. He was a very safe friend to have. We only had a couple of drinks because I had dinner plans with my mom. I still felt like a kid: "I have to go because my mom is waiting for me." I wanted to stay and drink more. I was crawling out of my skin. I wanted to get so fucked-up and ask Jeff a ton of questions and meet more strangers and do something crazy, but I had to meet my mom. Jeff told me to keep in touch and to call him if I needed anything. Oh, and he paid. Score. I loved being a girl because I knew that I had power over men and could get things from them.

I'm Jeff - I'm nice and normal and have a steady job

I'm Amber and I won't have sex with you unless you develop a drug problem or something

I wasn't having any luck finding a comfortable living situation. My budget was only six hundred bucks a month, and I had no idea this meant I'd have to live either in a borough, or in a closet in Manhattan. But finding a job was easy. It was 1999, the dot-com world was booming, Clinton was president, and there were plenty of jobs for recent college grads.

I ended up landing a gig as a headhunter at a place called JobbyJobs.com (I made that name up) down in the Wall Street area on John Street. I wore the power suit my mom had bought me to the interview, and quickly realized I was way overdressed. But if I'm being honest, that suit made me feel very powerful, even if I did look like an idiot. I stood up straight, and I walked real fast. I even bought a briefcase and put snacks in there.

During the interview I tried to pretend that I knew what a headhunter was, but the guy who interviewed me was more impressed that I played basketball in college than anything else. He offered me the job on the spot and said I could start on Monday. I was like, "Uh. Okay." I was going to be the only woman in the office. I was okay with that because guys are always nice to girls because they want to have sex with us. Then after they have sex with us, they are mean to us. Anyway, he introduced me to everyone, and my favorite was this Irish guy named Joe. He was so cute and charming, and he talked real fast. Tall, skinny, dark hair, blue eyes, with a big smile that revealed one crooked tooth. I got butterflies in my stomach and formed a crush on him before I even shook his hand.

The first week flew by, and it was time for my mom and her friends to leave. It was a Friday. I started my new job on Monday, and I still hadn't found a place to live. I didn't want to stay in the hotel because it was really expensive. My mom kept asking me if I was going to be okay. I was like, "Yeah. I'll be fine. I'll just call that stranger I met on the Internet and stay with him." She cried one more time as she hugged me good-bye. Then she walked out the door with her motley crew of friends who were going on and on about what a good time they had, while she was probably thinking that her oldest daughter was going to die.

I had a few more hours in the hotel before checkout time, and it felt very weird being all alone. I wished my mom and her chatty friends would come back. Tears started to roll down my cheeks, and I wanted them to stop. I looked in the mirror, channeled Tony Robbins, and told myself, "You can do this. Everything is going to be okay. You can do anything you set your mind to." Then I called Jeff and begged him to let me stay with him for a couple of nights.

While I was waiting for him to pick me up on the corner of a numbered street and a numbered avenue, I spotted a bright-yellow free classifieds newspaper called *The Loot*. I picked one up and put it in my backpack, I wanted to check out every roommate option I could. I did not want to be a burden on Jeff for long.

I hated asking for help; it made me so uncomfortable. Asking for help has always felt like a commitment. I assumed that if someone helped me I was going to have to pay them back, or they'd want something in return from me. Eww. No way. It was just easier for me to do everything on my own but, in this case, I *had* to ask for help. Jeff was my only lifeline.

REMAINING LIFE LINES

~~CALL FAMILY TO SAVE ME~~ ~~MAYBE JUST LIVE UNDER A HOTEL BED~~ BEG A STRANGER FOR HELP

When he finally arrived, a sense of relief washed over me. He jumped out of his car and waved both hands in the air to make sure I saw him, and I thought, "This guy is cool." I lugged both of my suitcases across the street and dumped them in his trunk. I gave him a hug, hoping he knew that this was a hug of appreciation, not attraction. We drove over the Triborough Bridge to get to his apartment in Astoria, Queens.

The view, the traffic, and the busyness of it all was so overwhelming. My excitement would turn to fear all in the same minute. I'd feel optimistic, thinking things would work out; then one negative thought would enter my mind, and I'd spin out in a spiral of fear. Everything was so loud and big, and my small-town senses had not adjusted yet. I was like a mouse in a factory that made big gigantic ceramic cats, nothing to be afraid of really, but it was still scary.

Jeff's place was nice, and it was bigger than the places I looked at in Manhattan. It was pretty clean. When he opened up the fridge to grab a beer, I didn't see any severed heads, and that was a relief. He had a roommate, an Asian girl who didn't speak much English, and she pronounced my name "Ambird." Jeff thought this was so hilarious. I was like, "It's a little funny, but not that funny." I was worried about his sense of humor.

As it turns out, he was a huge beer-drinking, computer-programming pothead who loved to build databases. All weekend we drank bottles of Bud, smoked pot, and stared at his computer screen. I pretended to care about his passion for programming. But in my mind, I was like, "I want to go dancing or something. This is my first weekend on my own in New York. I don't want to watch him type his clients' names into square boxes." But he was so stoned and excited to show me his programming skills I didn't have the heart to tell him I was bored and would rather be raging at a club. He was saving my ass by letting me stay with him, so I did what he wanted, and that was staring at a computer screen. I just smiled and said "That's cool" about four hundred times.

I slept on a futon in his living room and was so thankful he didn't hit on me or try anything weird. I got SO STONED all weekend I didn't even feel like drinking that much and started to wonder if maybe I should be a computer programmer. Whenever I got super, super stoned, it curbed my craving to drink because I already felt so fucked-up.

I thought about the last time I was this stoned with Lisa and how we drove straight into that tornado. It made me laugh and made me miss my old life in Pueblo. I started to think about my new life and wished I wasn't so stoned in that moment. In certain situations, weed made me overthink everything, which was not good because I naturally overthink everything. Stoners would tell me, "Smoke the Indica strain. It'll chill you out." I was like, "Okay," but was always so stoned when they told me that I'd forget to smoke that type of weed and would just smoke whatever was handed to me. And now here I was stoned out of my mind in Queens with a strange man the day before I started my first big job.

I started to freak out; paranoia was setting in. I felt irresponsible because I didn't have my own place yet. I tried to stop being stoned. "Stop being so high," I told myself. I needed to do something responsible. So I opened up *The Loot*, and a listing popped out at me. *$650 private room in Astoria, Queens.* I read the address aloud to Jeff, and he said that was just a few blocks away from his place. I called the number, and a man with a very thick Columbian accent answered. I told him my situation and he said I could come check out the place now if I wanted. A half hour later I was sitting on a white leather couch in his living room, still stoned, still paranoid.

His name was Louis. He'd just been through a divorce, and he had only been living in the States for a few years. He asked me a bunch of questions, and after each one of my answers, he would nod real slowly. I was being as friendly and as smiley as I possibly could, wondering if he could smell weed on me. I wanted the room. The apartment was bigger than the crapholes I looked at in Manhattan, and it was real clean. Plus, Jeff was just a few blocks away! If I ever wanted to get stoned and stare at a computer database, I just had to walk down the street! At the end of our "interview," Louis said I could move in right away if I wanted. He said he had interviewed thirty people already and liked me the most. I was very flattered and moved in that night.

Jeff drove me and my two suitcases over to what would be my first apartment in NYC. He said to keep in touch, let's hang out again soon, and be careful. I thanked him about a gazillion times, walked into my new apartment, chatted with Louis for a little bit (I could tell he wanted to talk more but I kept it short), and got settled into my partially furnished room. I could not believe I'd done it. I had officially moved. I called my mom and told her the good news.

I could hardly sleep that night. The bed in my room was not that comfortable, and I kept thinking about that cute boy Joe who I'd be working with starting tomorrow. My mind was racing: What was I going to wear? What is a headhunter? Who is the Columbian guy sleeping in the room next to me?

MY NEW ROOM IN ASTORIA QUEENS

I can't believe I am here I am so excited and scared and happy and sad

Wonder if I am going to be successful at something or if I am going to get murdered We'll see!

Okay, wait. I just had this moment where I'm wondering if you're thinking, "Okay, congratulations. You moved to New York and you're excited about it, but when does it get dark? Isn't this a book about alcoholism?" Well, I'm happy to announce that my downward spiral begins very soon. I just wanted to share this first week with you in detail because it felt weird to be like, "I moved from Pueblo to NYC and I didn't have a job or an apartment, and then I started drinking a lot. The End. Bye." I wanted you to know that my mom was so worried about me but didn't discourage me from going. I wanted you to know how determined I was to make this move work and how being naive, stupid, and open-minded helped me navigate my way into a secure spot without being murdered or sucked into a cult. And once I settled in, I was ready to party really fucking hard.

I had experimented enough with alcohol to know that I loved it very much. I loved the way it made me feel, but I think most of all, I loved how it made me NOT feel. My years dedicated to being a disciplined student, athlete, and overall human had suppressed my rage and my wild side and my overall desire to be crazy. As I laid there thinking about who I was and where I came from and where I was going, I wanted to explode. I was about to start my big corporate gig the next day. I was also about to go on a nine-year bender.

Chapter Six

My binge drinking began immediately with the boys I worked with down on Wall Street. I like saying "down on Wall Street" because it sounds like we were evil and rich, but we just worked in the Wall Street area. The guys that I worked with were broke dudes from Jersey who liked sports, beer, and girls, and just wanted to close some headhunting deals so they could pay their rent. I discovered that a headhunter is someone who finds another person a job; we didn't have those in Pueblo.

Literal Head hunting

We worked on commission, but they did give us a small weekly salary. I hated it. We had to cold call CEOs of Internet companies and pitch them potential employees, mostly web designers and software engineers. There were only a couple of computers in the office. I didn't get one because I was new, and the boss man said, "You get a computer when you close a deal." I wanted a computer so bad; I loved sending e-mails and searching the World Wide Web for information. But all I got was a desk with a phone like it was the '80s or something. I couldn't even pronounce half the words in the script they gave me to say to these people. Sometimes I'd hang up on them after they said hello because I didn't want to bother them.

Joe, the cute Irish guy I had a crush on, made this job exciting because he didn't give a fuck and everything was a joke to him. He was the funniest person I had ever met, and I became slightly obsessed with him. He was close friends with two other guys in the office: Pat, a rosy-cheeked Irish kid who was my age, and Dan, a middle-aged Jewish man who always looked me up and down and then say I looked cute. I thought he was gross but always said thanks when he complimented my looks.

When they'd invite me out for drinks after work, my drinking strategy was this: drink as many drinks as fast as possible and then see what happens. I had to get drunk right away because I felt very uncomfortable socializing with these guys. I thought they were so much smarter than me, even though they were your typical sports-lovin', women-lovin' men. They seemed so sophisticated and quick-witted. I knew it was because they grew up in a big city and were exposed to so much more than what people on farms are exposed to. Their minds were so fast. They talked about movies, books, authors, filmmakers, politicians, and places

I had never even heard of. I felt like I had nothing to add to these conversations and quickly adopted the role of the cute, dumb girl. I hated this about myself, but it worked. They liked me because all I would do is smile and flirt and dish out fake compliments. The booze made me forget that I felt dumb; it gave me a lot of confidence and it inspired things for me to say. After I slammed a few drinks, I was able to ask questions, change the subject, or tell a story.

I'd get drunk with these guys a few nights a week, usually at a bar in the Financial District, then take the hour-long train ride back to Queens. Sometimes I'd pass out and miss my stop and wake up and have no idea where I was. I'd simply walk off the train, cross the platform, and get on a train going back the direction I came from and hope they'd stop at my stop. I wouldn't get home until four or five in the morning, and I'd have just enough time to take a shower and head back to work. This was okay with me because I was still riding the high of moving. I was doing it! I was a New Yorker! Who cares if I was getting wasted all of the time and putting myself in dangerous situations and peeing behind Dumpsters and asking the homeless people behind the Dumpsters to look away while I squatted. I was a big-city girl.

One night, after drinking with the boys from work, I went wandering around the West Village. I made eye contact with a super cute boy in the street and started to talk to him. He had a thick accent. I don't know what kind of accent. All I knew was that English was not his first language, and I liked that we had hard a time communicating. I told him I wanted sushi because I tried it for the first time the week before and I loved it. We went to a ouchi restaurant and ate a bunch of raw fish and drank a lot and I remember feeling so connected to him. The next thing I remember is waking up next to him in a cab in front of my apartment, and I didn't understand why he was with me. I was like, "You can't come into my apartment. I have to go." He said, "You invited me over to your house." I said, "Well, I changed my mind," then I got out and slammed the door. Sometimes I did the most bizarre shit.

During these first few months in NYC, the guys in the office were my only friends. Well, besides Jeff, who I'd still see once in a while but not often. I felt a little guilty about being like, "Thanks for saving me when I first moved here. BYE!" I thought I had to be his friend because he was so nice to me, but we had nothing in common. I could not stand staying in at night, and he hated the bar scene. I wanted to explore everything, and he wanted to stay home on his computer. So our contact with each other slowly faded. Louis, my roommate, wanted to hang out, but I avoided him because it made me nervous that he wanted to get close to me. I just wanted to pay rent, come and go as I pleased, and not feel guilty about not inviting him out on my drinking sprees. I kept my distance; he was starting to creep me out. I thought maybe he wasn't interviewing people to be his roommate. Maybe he was interviewing them to be his girlfriend. VOMIT.

The only person I wanted to get close to was Joe. I couldn't tell if he liked me or not, or maybe he wasn't aware of how much I liked him. He was a bit of a mystery at first, but then it was slowly revealed that he was nuts. I think he knew he was nuts and was keeping his distance to save me from him. He has what I like to the call "the crazy switch." It's when someone turns into a completely different version of themselves when they drink. I mean we're all different when we drink, but people with the crazy switch do a 180. When Joe was sober, he was really silly and fun and thoughtful. When he was drunk, the light in his eyes disappeared, the structure of his face changed, and sometimes he got really mean. You'd think this would stop me from liking him, but . . . nope. It only fueled my desire to save him. I thought, "He is way too talented and smart to be ruining his life by drinking too much," as I slammed back multiple cocktails completely unaware of the irony.

I made it very clear that I wanted to hang out with Joe and be around him a lot. He finally started inviting me over to his new place in Jersey City. He had just moved in with Pat and Dan. They had a huge three-bedroom apartment with an incredible view of Manhattan, but they didn't have ANY furniture. They all slept on the floor. I thought, "Okay, well, they just moved in, they'll get furniture eventually." Nope. A few weeks went by and there was still no furniture, but I didn't really care. The first time Joe and I had sex was the last time, because . . . just keep reading . . . is this a thrilling cliff-hanger or what?

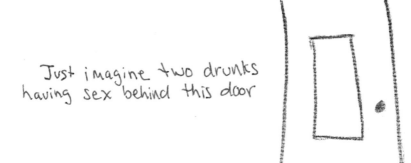

I was changing a lot during this time. Everything I was exposed to was different, big, challenging, exciting, and scary; my life back in Colorado felt like a dream. I'd call my family every once in a while to check in, but I felt very distant from them. There was no way any of them could understand or comprehend my new life, so I never revealed too much information. The truth was I was binge drinking every night, dating an alcoholic, and hating my job. But I told them everything was going great and I was having a lot of fun. And I thought I was having fun because when I was drunk it felt good. Being high on whatever your drug of choice is feels great, and that's why it's easy to convince yourself your life is great until you wake up and hate everything.

A couple months after moving, I started to panic about what I was doing with my life. I didn't want to be a headhunter! I didn't move to NYC to find other people their dream jobs. I wanted a dream job; I just didn't know what it was. My twentysomething angst of "What am I gonna do with my life?" took over my nervous system and fueled my discomfort. I secretly wanted to be a comedic actress, but I had no idea how to do that. And I didn't want to tell people this because I thought it was too lofty and stupid or delusional. I kept this dream to myself because maybe if I admitted it, I would have to do something about it, and that was scary to me. I was willing to move to New York by myself but couldn't admit that I wanted to be a funny actress. I channeled bravery and fear in weird ways, and I just didn't have the guts to deal with that goal. Drinking helped me cope with this.

Work was getting worse. The morale in the office was low; no one was closing deals. Joe would go on these massive drinking benders and miss days of work. He called from jail a couple of times. I hadn't seen him much since the night we had sex, and I realized that maybe I shouldn't love him so much because he was very fucked-up. I loved to save people, but I couldn't save people who were always in jail. I would leave that up to the law.

The jury finds you guilty of trying to save a man who can't be saved you are sentenced to breaking up with him.

One night, I got to see Joe's insanity unfold right before my eyes. Prior to this, I'd see him get loud and rude and maybe pick a fight. I'd see him go from fun-lovin' and funny to rude and obnoxious over the course of a few drinks, but this night was different. Me, Pat, and Joe went for drinks after work like we had a hundred times before. (Dan stopped hanging out with us because Joe got on his nerves, and I was okay with this because Dan got on my nerves.) We went to the dive bar across the street, pounded as many as we could during happy hour, then took the PATH train to Jersey City. Joe seemed fine—drunk and a little obnoxious but nothing out of the ordinary. Pat was drunk. I was drunk. It was fun!

It was raining that night, and Joe had a big umbrella with him. When we got off the train in Jersey City, there was a homeless man sitting up against the train-station wall. He asked us for change, and when we didn't give him any, he murmured something under his breath. I couldn't understand him and didn't think anything of it. Another night, another homeless person. I was desensitized, drunk, and didn't care.

We all kept walking, but then Joe suddenly stopped, as if he just realized he had forgotten something. He calmly turned around and walked back toward the homeless guy. He slowly raised his umbrella up in the air and proceeded to beat him. I couldn't believe what I was seeing. He'd lift the umbrella up and WHAM slam it down on him. Lift it up again and WHAM slam it down on him. The homeless man was curled up in a ball, protecting his face from the blows. Pat and I were screaming, "JOE. STOP. STOP IT! LEAVE HIM ALONE." We ran over, and Pat tried to pull Joe off. I just stood there in shock like, "Jesus Christ. Joe is so fucked-up. I hope he doesn't kill him." Joe took a swing at Pat every time he tried to stop him. I could hear police sirens in the distance and prayed they were coming for us.

They were; there must have been security cameras because they got there fast. The cops whipped into the train-station parking lot, jumped out of their car, and pounced on Joe. Pat told me to run. I felt like I was in a movie, and I was a bad guy, even though I was on the homeless man's side. I was a bad good guy! One of the cops ran after me and told me to stop. I froze and was like, "Hi." He asked me what happened, and I just told him what I knew, "My friend beat that homeless man with an umbrella because he gets crazy when he drinks alcohol." The police officer asked if I had been drinking, and I said no. I looked over, and Joe was in handcuffs. The other officer was talking to Pat. They hauled Joe off to jail.

I walked with Pat the rest of the way to their apartment. I was gonna sleep on the floor alone that night, and that was okay with me. I never wanted to see Joe again. I asked Pat why he thought Joe acted like that. He said something like, "He just gets nuts when he drinks. He just . . . I don't know. He just goes crazy." It made me think about my drinking and how under control I was. Joe's insane relationship with alcohol made my relationship with alcohol look very innocent and even healthy.

After this happened, I kept my distance from Joe. We loved each other, but we had an understanding that we couldn't take each other seriously because we were both nuts in our own special way. I was looking for a new job and wanted to remove myself from this environment completely. Out of nowhere, I got an e-mail from a guy named Chad. I had heard of him before. The guys in the office would talk about him, "Oh yeah, when Chad used to work here he'd blah blah blah." I'm not sure how he got my e-mail address, but he wrote, "Hey. I used to work at JobbyJobs.com and started my own company. I know it blows there, so if you want a new job, send me your résumé. I'll blast it to a bunch of Internet start-ups."

Within a week, I had set up several interviews. Employers would e-mail me, "Hello, I received your résumé and would love to meet with you." Chad said he sent my résumé out to over 500 companies with his new spam system. I went on a lot of interviews and ended up getting a new job as a marketing associate at an Internet start-up, but had a few other offers from other companies. I couldn't believe how easy it was to find a job in this town.

I wanted to thank him for helping me, so I invited him out for some drinks. We gossiped about JobbyJobs.com. He talked a lot about how crazy Joe was, and I didn't want him to know that I dated him. Everyone knew he was so messed up, and I'm the dummy who dated him. I hated myself. This shame made me want to drink and I did. I ended up getting super wasted that night. I wanted Chad to like me, and I thought I owed him something. I thought he was so cool for starting his own company and teaching himself how to spam people. The Internet was so new, and he already figured it out. He's way better than Joe. I better let him touch my body or something.

I remember playing pool and being really bad at it. Normally, I could at least hit a corner-pocket shot, but I could barely stand up. Chad was a shark; he was so good. I think he enjoyed beating me. He had this bully quality to him. I also remember him handing me a pill and telling me to take it. I took it without questioning what it was. I blacked out and woke up lying next to him the next morning, in MY bed. I had no idea how we got home. I must've told him where I lived because he had never been to my place before. My clothes were still on, including my jacket, so I prayed nothing had happened.

We didn't say much to each other that morning, probably because were both so hungover and I was busy trying to piece together the rest of the night. The last thing I remember was being at the bar playing pool. I didn't want to ask him what happened because I didn't want him to know how fucked-up I was (as if he didn't know). Maybe it's better that I didn't remember; maybe he just wanted to make sure I got home all right. My way of rationalizing was, "Well, at least he's better than the last guy, even though he beat me at pool, then told me to take a pill." He and I e-mailed a few times after that, but I never saw him again. I thought nothing of it. I chalked it up to "I'm a party girl, just having fun."

Blackout: A Momentary loss
of consciousness
or
Partial or total loss
of memory
Damn Man ... I Don't know
what happened

Chapter Seven

I was nervous about my new job. I got hired as an entry-level marketing associate for an Internet start-up whose target market was Magic: The Gathering players. It's like poker for dorks. They considered themselves "the online destination for gamers." I'll just call it PokerForDorks.com. A handful of young Ivy League Asian kids launched this site and had just received millions of dollars from an investor in Florida.

The office space was the CEO's apartment, just a block west of Times Square. I sat at a table in the living room with a bunch of programmers who were socially awkward, but kind. I felt out of place because everyone had known each other for years. They were a group of young geniuses who had started a company together, and they had a special bond. They had just started to hire "outside people," and I was one of the lucky ones. I immediately felt like they had made a mistake hiring me because I had no idea what I was doing, and all I wanted was for everyone to like me.

My direct boss was the director of marketing, Liza. She was a tiny, feisty, Filipino lady in her early thirties. She was a Yale graduate and had the coolest pixie haircut and black framed glasses. She had worked in TV production on

Xena: Warrior Princess. Her boyfriend was a tall, thin, white, bald guy who ran a satirical political website. I thought all of this was incredible. Liza loved to party and openly talked about her sexual adventures and would boss the boys around in the office. I both loved and feared her.

She was confident and didn't kiss anyone's ass; she even thought some of the guys in the office were idiots. I loved this because I put everyone on a pedestal. It was refreshing when she called these top-notch college graduates dumb asses. It made me realize maybe not everyone was smarter than me. Plus, she'd tell me *I* was smart. I thought maybe she felt sorry for me, and that's why she said that. Compliments from people I admired made me nervous. I was way more comfortable when people underestimated me because it was easy to impress them. But the second I impressed them, their expectations went up, which meant I couldn't be a loser. It's hard being a winner! And sometimes when I did accept a compliment, I'd let it go to my head. I'd fluctuate between feeling like a worthless piece of shit or like I was better than everyone—nothing in between.

You are Smart

Ok great now I am going to act like a cocky asshole

In the beginning, this job was great. I learned about marketing and PR, and I also had the freedom to do whatever I wanted. My favorite thing was how I could indulge in my obsession with the Internet. I had limited access to it because I didn't have my own computer at home, and I always had to go to libraries and other places where you had to pay to get online. Now I had my own office and my own computer, and I'd spend hours looking at cool new websites, researching our competitors, and coming up with fun ways to interact with our users. I thought I was finally putting my business degree to work and I felt important.

I'd think about being a comedic actress every day, but I still wasn't ready to admit it. I would deal with that later. Besides, it was a magical time in NYC because everyone had money and a job. Everyone was creating websites and ways to make money on the Internet. The world was changing, and I felt lucky to be a part of it.

I quickly gained confidence in navigating the city at night and had no problem going to bars alone or saying yes to random invitations to parties and events. I loved talking to strangers and my drinking felt way more sophisticated than when I drank with the boys from JobbyJobs.com. Those boys were sloppy and dramatic and didn't have any life goals. Now I was drinking with creative and motivated people. They didn't beat up homeless people, and they talked about their ideas, dreams, and what they were working on.

When I first started to go bars by myself, I'd drink a lot real fast, get a buzz, then try to meet a random person. I wanted to meet boys, girls, old people, young people—it didn't matter—I just wanted to connect. And not in a sexual way. I just wanted to meet new people and explore new opportunities. I was drawn to the night, as if the moon was a magnet that wouldn't let me go. I'm trying to be poetic; I hope you love it. What I'm trying to say is, I felt like I was seeking something that I didn't fully understand. I was seeking something to fill a void that no drink or person could ever fill, but I thought it could. This feeling was powerful, and it kept me in bars until closing time almost every single night.

I was always hungover at work, but since I was young I bounced back pretty quickly. And my need to please people drove me to show up and work hard. I was slowly becoming friends with the Ivy Leaguers in the office. At first, I didn't hang out with them because they'd stay late in the office/apartment and play Magic: The Gathering or computer games like *Warcraft* or *Tomb Raider* and I was like, "Um. Bye." But once we used some of the money we got from the investors to move into a big new office in Koreatown, we started to have small office parties.

Someone would go on a booze run around 5 p.m., and we'd all gather around and start drinking and talking. It was supposed to be innocent and mellow, but one time I got so wasted I ended up passing out under my desk. I just had no control over how much I drank. You'd think at some point I'd just stop picking up drinks and pouring them into my mouth. But I drank without thinking about it. Once I realized how drunk I was, it was too late. My only option was to lie down and go to sleep.

I woke up the next morning, and it was already time for work. I guess no one noticed I was passed out under my desk because I was still there. I ran out and bought a toothbrush, grabbed a bagel and some coffee, ran back to the office, and put on one of the company T-shirts we kept stashed in the marketing closet. Mike, a nosy coworker who was always asking me questions about everything, asked me if I had slept in the office. I was like, "Yes, but if you tell anyone I'll cut you." He thought it was hilarious. I sort of did too, but was bummed someone in the office knew about it.

We eventually started splurging on nights out on the town, mostly at Korean karaoke places. The CEO, Stan, who I thought was very cute and mature and sophisticated, would get us a private room and order bottle after bottle of whatever booze we wanted. He had the best skin and was sort of quiet. But you could tell he was a man with a plan, and I loved that he didn't need to be the center of attention. He was the silent warrior type. I thought this was very sexy. I'd try to get him to notice me all of the time, not only because I wanted validation from the big boss but because I wanted him to want me.

These karaoke nights were incredible. We were just a bunch of Internet dorks raging until 4 a.m., young, motivated, hopeful, and scream-singing as loud as we could. We'd stand on the couches, put our arms around each other, sway back and forth, and sing Bon Jovi, ABBA, Cher, the classics—it was the best. These nights made binge drinking okay. It was fun, relatively safe, and it was a great way for me to get closer to my coworkers. Without these nights out together, I would have always been on the outside of the group. But since they liked to party with me, I felt like I was finally one of them.

Stan eventually asked me out on an official date; he probably couldn't get my tone-deaf karaoke singing out of his head. He was hesitant and felt so guilty asking me out because he was my boss. It was sort of cute how he cared about this, but I was like, "Who gives a shit? We're all gonna die, Stan. Let's go out." He took me to a fancy dinner, then to the Broadway show, *Fosse*. It was incredible. That show blew my mind out of my skull.

Afterward, we went back to his place. I wasn't drunk enough to handle this situation and got very nervous because over the course of the night, I had decided that I wasn't attracted to him. He was so normal and stable, and this grossed me out. Where was the drama, the mystery, the humor you develop because of your tragic life or twisted and sick perspective? He had none of this! So, when we were making out in his bed, I told him that I had to go to the bathroom. I needed to plan my escape. I walked out of his bedroom and saw a bottle of vodka on the kitchen counter and just started slamming it. Like, gulping it *Leaving Las Vegas*–style à la Nicolas Cage.

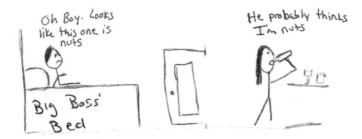

While I was doing this, I thought to myself, "This is crazy. This is not normal," but I just kept drinking. Then I went to pee, and it smelled funny. That fancy dinner had asparagus in it! The bitter stank that was wafting up from my vagina made me wish I could travel back in time and order broccoli. When I finally made it back to the bedroom, he started kissing me right away. He took off my clothes and started to go down on me. I panicked because I knew what it smelled like down there. Plus, I still wasn't attracted to him! The vodka didn't make me horny; it just made my head spin. I was like, "Stop. I don't want to do this." He stopped. I told him I wasn't ready, and I just wanted to go to bed. I passed out and left early the next day. We "broke up" a week later.

No I'm not attracted to you because you're normal and my vagina smells like a vegetable

Come closer

Thankfully, I was able to take a break from the awkward "I hooked up with the boss man and now it's weird in the office" vibes because it was time to go home for Christmas. It would be my first trip back home since I moved. When I got to Pueblo, I acted sort of snobby. I dressed all in black (my new thing) and judged everyone who had never moved away. Everyone seemed so slow and boring to me, same old, same old. I thought about taking a break from drinking when I was home, but it was impossible. Booze was everywhere, and it was mostly free. I'd go to the Do Drop and saddle up to the bar, just like the men I used to watch drink when I was a kid. If I didn't recognize the bartender, I'd say, "I'm the owner's daughter" and get whatever I wanted. I met up with friends and drank to get drunk.

I loved seeing people I went to high school with so I could brag about moving to New York. Tammy-Lou, remember her from the first chapter? Well, she had grown up to be hot shit in Pueblo. We were really good friends for a long time. I always loved her and her family. They were well known and wealthy, and she was practically Pueblo royalty. Some quiet competition had developed between us over the years, and I felt like my move to New York was more fancy than anything she had ever done. She was rich and popular, but at least I got outta that place. I also drank with my mom and her friends, the ladies who dropped me off in that Midtown hotel just a few months before. They wanted to hear all about my adventures and said nice things to me. I thought they were so impressed that I got a job working at an Internet company and lived with a strange Colombian man.

Life Choices Award

1st Place
Moved to NYC
by herself and
moved in with
a stranger and
drinks a lot

2nd Place
Stayed in Pueblo
to be with
her family

3rd Place
Got a neck
tattoo

Our family holiday parties were always stocked with wine, hard liquor, beer, and spiked eggnog. These drinks were just an arm's reach away. Often times a family member came around asking if you needed a refill. The only one who seemed out of control, with an obvious drinking problem, was my uncle Woody. We worried about him, but we loved and accepted him. He was hilarious and ridiculous. He'd spend most of his time in the garage chain-smoking, laughing, and pouring shots for whoever would sneak back there because they knew he'd give them a shot. My mom and aunts liked to party, but they'd just get a little buzzed and stop drinking. They aren't alcoholics. My grandma would get tipsy once or twice a year off blackberry brandy, and the rest of the time she wouldn't "touch the stuff."

It was easy for me to fly under the radar during the holidays because there were so many people around; cousins and kids and babies and extended family members and friends of friends would stop by, so I'd blend in and drink a lot without anyone noticing. I'd just slowly get shitfaced over the course of the night and pass out wherever I laid down, and that was okay because we were family! If I ended up sleeping in my clothes on my aunt Sabrina's couch, that was okay. That didn't seem crazy. It just seemed like I slept on my aunt's couch with my clothes on. No big deal.

I made it back to my mom's house on Christmas morning and was so hungover. Too much food, too much booze, too much family. After I handed out the cheap gifts I bought for my mom and siblings in Chinatown, I'd lay around all day until it was time to go see my dad with Adam and Autumn. My mom and grandma would always make us take him a plate of food on Christmas Day. "Here, take this to your dad," they'd say and hand us plates packed with food. I always thought it was cool how my mom wanted to make sure he had a nice meal on Christmas even though he was a terrible husband and father. Classy.

My dad was usually either living with his mom (my grandma Tozer who I wasn't that close to) or in a small, crappy apartment. He lost the house we grew up in somehow after the divorce; we're not sure how. It was almost paid off, so maybe he sold it and blew the money? Wherever he was living, I never liked to stay long. We'd exchange worthless little gifts. He'd complain so much about everything. I'd get quiet and count down the minutes until I felt like I had spent enough time with him, so I could leave without feeling too guilty about it.

Adam spent the most time with my dad. He took the brunt of the annoying chore that my father had turned into. He'd help him move, make sure he had food, visit him, and just make sure he was okay, but he was not okay. Autumn was a preteen, too young to take on his problems, and I chose to separate myself from him as much as possible. The second I would engage with my dad or even think about him, I'd fill up with anger and then internalize it. My rage was in a cage in the pit of my stomach, and all I could do was kill it with alcohol for short periods of time.

When I went back to work after the holidays, I felt *blah*. Maybe it was the constant cold East Coast weather, or the fact that the company was losing money and we stopped doing karaoke, or that I was no longer impressed or intimidated by the Ivy Leaguers. I was bored. The rush of learning something new was over. The flirtatious fire between Stan and me had been scorched by my asparagus vagina and preference in broken men, so there was nothing to look forward to at work anymore. My routine became predictable. I was either at work, getting drunk, or hungover. I hated sitting at my desk all day, shaky and tired from the night before. I felt like I was rotting.

Since my coworkers stopped partying after work, I had to find other ways to drink, besides going to bars by myself. I got so desperate for social opportunities, I started to hang out with my creepy roommate Louis once in a while. One night, we went to a Russian dance club in Queens, where I danced with everyone but him. I was nervous about leading him on, so I made sure to act like a megabitch so he'd know the deal. Communicating like an honest adult was not an option; only passive aggressive behavior would do.

What is the best way to communicate with other humans?

☐ open and honestly

☑ passive aggressively with self seeking motives and don't forget to lie a lot

Another night we went to his friend's party at an apartment on the Upper East Side. There were about fifteen people crammed into the kitchen and living room that was also the bedroom. I loved going to people's apartments in the city. Their living spaces were always really small, packed with stuff from their life, creatively placed in nooks and crannies. Everyone was nice and chatty, but I still felt less than everyone else. I felt stupid and clueless, so I of course had to drink my way through it. I did my usual routine, just slowly getting drunker and drunker throughout the night. If I felt uncomfortable in a conversation, I'd drink more, hoping the confidence would show up soon.

There were two girls there who I thought were so cool. The way they dressed, the way they talked, the way they were slightly inappropriate and laughing a lot. They reminded me of the way Lisa and I were. Funny and loud, like they were putting on a show. As it turns out, they were a comedy duo—Ahna and Lauren. I was like, "Wow. They are comedic actresses. They are who I want to be." I was in awe of them all night long, soaking up everything they did while ignoring Louis. At the end of the night, Ahna gave me a comedy flyer and said I should come to their show. I couldn't believe they had their own comedy-show flyers! I was so impressed and thought about them the whole train ride back home to Queens with Louis. He was trying to talk to me, and I just wanted him to stop trying.

I started thinking about comedy a lot more. The obsession of "what am I gonna do with my life, I wish I was doing comedy, it doesn't feel right working in this office" consumed my thoughts. I was becoming increasingly dissatisfied: "I don't care about gaming! I don't even know how to play Magic: The Gathering! How can I be passionate about something I don't understand! The boys who play these games need to take a shower and get laid!" I was slipping into a deep, dark depression, and that's when I decided I was going to go to that comedy show. I found that comedy flyer and went to that fucking show all by myself. I liked to do things by myself because when I invited people out with me, I felt responsible for their happiness, and it was just easier to be alone. Besides, comedy was something I wanted to explore on my own. I wanted to study it.

I stopped at a bar for a few drinks before I walked into the theater. I always liked to have a few drinks before I did anything at night because it got to the point where I couldn't do anything social without booze in my system. Their show was at a tiny, little theater, and I found a seat in the back corner. My eyes about popped out of my head when I watched them perform. I thought they were fantastic. It could have been the worst thing ever, but I was just amazed they had the guts to act silly onstage. It was my first alternative comedy show, and I just thought the fact that they were up there was incredible. I wanted so badly to be like them. They performed a few sketches and played different characters. Their humor wasn't like the stuff you'd see in a sitcom. It's like the stuff that made fun of sitcoms. Smart. They were these brave, creative warriors, and it made me wonder what it would take for me be a performer in New York City.

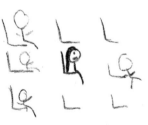

Oh my God they are amazing

Never sit on a man's face without his permission

Ahna + Lauren

Seeing the show snapped me out of my nine-to-five depression and inspired me to explore the comedy scene. It also showed me a new way to party. A new cycle had begun.

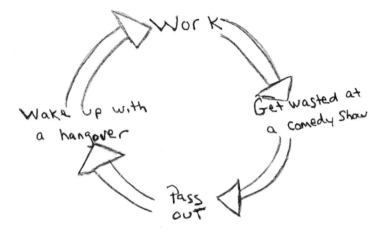

Chapter Eight

My hangovers were getting worse. It was taking longer for me to bounce back from a night of drinking. I'd try to go on jogs and eat healthy to counteract the amount of drinking I was doing, but I'd usually just walk around my neighborhood and have to go lie back down. This was scary to me because I used to be in great shape and could run for miles and miles. I told myself maybe I shouldn't drink so much. My first attempt at trying to control it was trying to not drink *every* night.

The one night I forced myself to not drink happened to be a night when Louis had some friends over to our apartment. I didn't have a drop of booze. I was proud of myself for being somewhat social while staying sober, but then Louis got drunk and really creeped me out. After his friends left he said, "I watch you, Amber. I watch you come in here late at night after you go out and party with your friends, and you don't spend time with me." I was like, "I AM YOUR ROOMMATE. I DON'T HAVE TO HANG OUT WITH YOU. I AM NOT YOUR GIRLFRIEND." Then I stormed off to bed.

The next morning I woke up and there was a note on my door written in

Spanish. I tried to read it for about five minutes, then finally admitted to myself that I didn't know Spanish. I took it to work to see if anyone could translate it; the secretary said she could. She looked at it for a minute and said, "He said he's sorry and he's in love with you." I was like, "Gross," and moved out a couple weeks later.

I moved to Crown Heights, Brooklyn, with some guys from work. Mike, the nosy and nice guy and this one mellow dude, Al, had a big three-bedroom apartment, and one of their roommates had just moved out. It was perfect timing! Brooklyn was way cooler than Queens, and my room was much bigger than the one I had in Astoria. Around the same time I moved to Brooklyn, PokerForDorks.com went under. All of a sudden there was no money; I think we spent it all on private Korean karaoke rooms. I was okay with this because it was weird working with Stan after our little fling. I felt bad for him because his dream company failed. The investors from Florida were so mad at him, but that was his problem, not mine! Adios, Ivy Leaguers! I'm a badass Brooklyn bitch now!

The cool thing was that when the company went under, they gave me a computer. They completely ran out of money and said, "We can't give you your last paycheck, but we can give you a computer." I was like, "I am the luckiest person alive." I wanted a computer so bad and Mike and Al helped me hook it up to the Internet in my bedroom. I loved hearing the screeching sound of the dial-up modem. It meant I was about to be connected to the World Wide Web in my own bedroom! No more checking my e-mail at libraries or friends' houses or waiting to get to the office. The world was in the computer box in my bedroom and it was badass.

Another thing that made me happy was the comedy scene. I was going to so many shows. I had met a lot of comics and kept track of their shows. I was in this weird social limbo. I no longer hung out with coworkers after work because I didn't have a job. I didn't know anyone who liked comedy as much as I did, so I just went to these shows by myself. I didn't care. I'd have a few drinks before I went anywhere, so I had plenty of confidence showing up solo. I'd just get tanked and talk to everyone.

Besides the increasingly weary hangovers, I didn't suffer too many consequences when I drank. I didn't have people telling me I was out of control or that I had a problem. This was probably because I was always surrounded by other drunks, so if I was obnoxious they were too wasted to notice. My behavior was not out of control. I wasn't like Joe or the belligerent people I'd kick out of the Do Drop. I was just happy and confident and very chatty.

I loved drinking with comedians and immersed myself in the "NYC alternative comedy scene." It was so cool it was uncool to use the word "alternative" but everyone did because it's the best word to describe it. There were a lot of different types of performers doing stand-up, sketch, and music, and it was all happening in small, little black box theaters and bars all over the city. It fascinated me. These people were so creative and courageous and didn't have full-time jobs, and they didn't care. They put their art first, and just made all of the logistical things in life work out somehow. I wanted to be like them. I didn't want to be a marketing associate or sit at a desk all day. I wanted to drink and write and turn my tragic thoughts into comedic gold, but I couldn't help but panic about being broke. This panic made me drink, and drinking costs money. HELLO.

I had to get another job. Liza had already landed a new fancy gig at an Internet marketing consulting firm, and she told me she would hire me as soon as she could, and sure enough, she did. Before I knew it, I had another nine-to-five job. There I was, once again, sitting in a chair looking at a computer, not knowing what the fuck was going on. I actually liked starting new jobs because I learned a lot in a short amount of time—whether it was a new industry or skill, I had to soak it up. It was stimulating. But now that I had comedy on the brain, it was hard for me to believe that a day job would bring me joy.

I was pretty good at PR. I loved stalking reporters and writing press releases and coming up with cool ways to get clients in the news. I started using humor to communicate with reporters. I'd write weird e-mails like, "Yo, Bob. I saw your article on E-commerce in the *Wall Street Journal*, and I loved your liberal use of the words *it* and *the* and *a* . . . thought you might be interested in X company." It worked! People would always write me back. I learned how to be refreshing in an oversaturated industry.

Liza wasn't my direct boss at this place; she worked more in business development and I was strictly PR. We'd see each other once in a while, but not much. I was cool with that because the women in my department were hilarious. I hung out with this girl Rhonda from Jersey, and everything was such a big deal to her—in a fun way. "Oh my fuckin' gawd, did you hear what Bob said today? He's outta his fuckin' mind!" And she'd chomp gum real loud and tell us about the crazy sex she had with her boyfriend and how one time he donkey-punched her. I said, "You guys have a donkey?" She said, "No. He just punched me in the back of the head when he was fuckin' me from behind." I was like "Oh. Okay. Right on."

Another friend I made was Nikki. She was the secretary, in her early twenties, quiet at work but loved to rage at night. She grew up in Manhattan, was an only child, and her parents owned a fancy hair salon. They had a one-bedroom apartment in Midtown and a big house in upstate New York or maybe somewhere in New Jersey. We partied together a lot. She was like me; she drank to get FUCKED-UP. Rhonda would have to catch the train to Jersey, so she'd leave at a decent hour, but Nikki and I would rage till the a.m. Even if we were just in her apartment, we'd get all fucked-up while binge watching *Sex and the City*. We both said we hated that show, but we couldn't stop watching it.

Nikki and I even took a two-week trip to Europe. It was my first time overseas, and I was very excited. Nikki was well traveled. She'd been to Europe many times, so this trip wasn't a big deal to her. My excitement annoyed her, which annoyed me, because how could I not be excited? Both my obnoxious excitement and her jaded grumpiness didn't matter once we got drunk. Drinking made both of us so happy, and we needed it to get along on this trip. We went to Italy, Switzerland, Germany, and Amsterdam, and our last stop was London. In Italy, I got so drunk I fell out of a cab, and it ran over my foot. Nikki had to drag me into the train station because I was just lying in the street. She fed me a McDonald's cheeseburger; it was so delicious. And the first thing I did when I was able to sit up and talk was buy some hash from some dudes with dirty hair.

In Germany, we got so wasted we brought two boys we met at a bar back to our hotel. The plan was to have sex with them. But I couldn't go through with it, and I just laid there. The guy I was supposed to hook up with was like, "Come on." I said, "Sorry." Nikki fooled around with her guy. I don't know exactly what they did because my head was buried in a pillow. After they left, she said we were so stupid and I agreed. Then we had a pizza delivered. It was the most disgusting pizza I have ever tasted.

By the time we got to Amsterdam, we were both exhausted. We spent most of our time at a bed-and-breakfast run by a sweet old gay man who made us weird eggs and beans for breakfast every morning. We spent a couple of days sleeping and recovering, but I did somehow manage to go on a date with some random boy I met at a bar. He took me to the movies and that was it. I was too tired to get to know him. I just wanted to go back to the bed-and-breakfast so I could sleep. Nikki slept for two days straight.

Then we took a mini cruise ship from Amsterdam to London where I got super wasted and played blackjack. Nikki got mad at me because when it was time to get off the boat and go through customs, I could barely walk. I had never been this sloppy before—usually I was very functional and hyper and chatty—but on this European vacation I was such a sloppy mess. Nikki was very annoyed. She decided to stay in London for a few more days while I went back to NYC.

It was back to the nine-to-five grind, but there was some exciting drama happening at work. Rumors were going around that our boss wasn't actually a twenty-seven-year-old with an MBA; instead, he was a twenty-three-year-old compulsive liar with a coke problem. That's hot! Of course I developed a crush on him.

When Nikki got back from London, she forgave me for being such a sloppy, drunk asshole, and we started partying together again. One night, she and I went over to the cokehead liar boss's place to have some drinks. I was very excited. I thought maybe I was going to make out with another CEO. We sat around his living room and drank oversize vodka drinks, and it wasn't long before he busted out the coke and started doing lines. Nikki was into it, and she knew exactly what she was doing. She snorted that white powder like they do in the movies—her head hovering over the table with a rolled-up dollar bill, starting off with a slow turn of the head following the line on the table until it disappears, then whipping her head up real quick. I admitted I had never done coke before, but they were so nice and showed me how to snort it up my nostrils. I felt okay. I got a boost of energy and got real chatty for about an hour, but then I just wanted to go to bed. The cokehead liar boss said I could sleep in his bed. I was like, "Oh yeah, he wants my body." But nothing happened. He slept on the other side of the bed, and he didn't even touch me.

Me: Sorry I was
      so obnoxious
Nikki: It's ok-wanna
      go and do a
      drug that makes
      people obnoxious?
Me: Yes

Of course it was awkward at work after this, but me doing coke with the boss wasn't much of a concern for anyone because he did coke with a lot of people. And the company was facing much bigger problems. The business was slowly going under, and I realized that Internet companies either died quickly, or exploded with success. We were dead.

But one day, before the company went entirely to hell, I was standing outside the CNN building in Midtown waiting for a client. We had booked them an interview on some daytime-news show, and I was there for moral support. So, I'm standing there and I hear this voice behind me, this undeniably familiar voice. At the same time I was turning around to get a look at the person who belonged to this voice, I remembered who it was and thought, "That's Tony Robbins's voice." Then a second later, there he was walking past me. TONY FUCKING ROBBINS! I couldn't believe it! I ran up to him and was talking a mile a minute. He was about eight feet tall.

That's Awesome!

You brainwashed me and then I moved to New York and started binge drinking

He asked me what I was doing that weekend. I thought maybe he wanted to bone me or something, but all he wanted was for me to go to his seminar in New Jersey. He gave me a card, told me to call the number on it, and said he'd give me two free tickets. I couldn't believe it. I told all my coworkers and friends about it and asked if they wanted to go. None of them wanted to! They thought Tony was a joke, an infomercial hack, a cheesy self-help guru who preyed on sad people. I was like, "He changed my life. And my aunt Pam said after she listened to his tapes, she quit smoking." I was a little embarrassed that they thought the guy I loved was a joke. But at the same time, I thought they were cynical, and if anyone could use some positive thinking tools, it was them! I went by myself, of course.

I rode a short bus from Port Authority with a bunch of middle-aged Tony Robbins groupies to the Continental Arena where the conference was being held. When I told them I met Tony on the street and he gave me free tickets, their heads about fell off of their bodies. They couldn't believe it. "I spent five hundred bucks for my ticket!" yelled a sixty-year-old woman who probably hated her life and needed a change. I thought about her worthless husband and how she probably put her career on hold for him, and now she was gonna make a comeback with Tony's help. I also thought that I should've scalped my extra ticket for four hundred bucks and was mad at myself for not trying to sell it.

The conference was incredible. Barbara Walters, Larry King, and Christopher Reeve (God rest his soul) opened up for Tony (he was the headliner), and they all told their stories of success and failure and sang Tony's praises. They loved his work. I sat in the middle of a bunch of corporate guys who didn't want to be there. Their company paid for them to go; it was part of their training. They were all making fun of Tony at the beginning, but within a few hours, Tony had everyone in the palm of his hand. We were screaming and jumping. At one point he played "You're Simply the Best" by Tina Turner, and every suit in that place was singing and crying and swaying back and forth with positivity and love. It was so much fun getting brainwashed like that.

This boost of positive and deep thinking was exactly what I needed. I knew that no matter how interesting my day job was, I'd always want something more. Tony really helped me get clear on my fears and my goals and what was holding me back. I asked myself a bunch of important questions, and I was also brimming with confidence.

When I went back to work the next day, I asked for a $10,000 raise and got it. I thought that was incredible and so hilarious. I just asked for it and said I deserved it—and my cokehead boss was like, "Okay." Maybe he gave it to me because, why not? The company wasn't going to be around much longer. Or, maybe he gave it to me because he felt bad for giving me coke. Or maybe he gave it to me because he was high. Or maybe, just maybe, he thought I deserved it. Who cares, what matters was—I had the guts to ask.

That same week I was drinking at a bar with Nikki and Rhonda, and we started talking to a guy and his friends. I knew this guy from somewhere . . . oh yeah, he was a comic. I saw him bomb a few weeks ago. I asked him, "Do you do comedy? I think I saw you last month at Boston Comedy Club." He said, "Oh god. That set was awful." Then he went on to tell me that he had only done it a couple of times, and he couldn't believe I was at one of his shows. I asked him a bunch of questions about it, then I mentioned that I wanted to try it. He told me that he took a stand-up comedy class, and it helped him get over his fear of getting onstage. He gave me the phone number of his teacher.

A comedy teacher? I didn't even know those existed. I called up Tommy and told him that I wanted to do comedy but was so scared. He explained that his class was one night a week for six weeks. And after the six weeks, I would get five minutes of stage time. His class was designed to help students work out a five-minute set and get them onstage. I thought, "This is perfect. I can do this." And before ya knew it, I was drunk in his class working out a five-minute comedy set.

I was thrilled to be taking some sort of action toward my goal. I had met so many stand-up comics, and I think they thought I was a groupie or something, even though I only made out with seven or ten of them. But I didn't feel like a hanger-on; I felt more like a student of comedy when I was at shows. I was studying them. And I didn't want to be just a fan; I wanted to be a fellow. I wanted to get onstage so bad, and Tommy's class was my ticket.

We'd meet once a week in a small theater near Times Square, and it made me feel creative, like I was a real artist. I'd always have a couple of drinks before I went to class because I *had* to. Drinks before doing anything related to comedy became my MO. It gave me that extra boost of confidence and relaxation that eluded me when I was sober. We started out the class by getting onstage and simply talking about our lives and what we thought was funny about ourselves.

I was like, "I don't know man, I just like to party, and I end up in these crazy situations." Most of the stuff I talked about was inspired by my party lifestyle. I didn't understand what a punch line was, and I sounded like I was on heroin.

There was a tall, red-headed guy named Stu who was always in class. He was Tommy's good friend and would sit in the back of the room and yell out possible punch lines for the students onstage, then laugh really hard at his own jokes. He was semiperverted but harmless, and he and I became quick friends. He was obsessed with British comedy and would always quote shows I had never seen, and I was like "haha" even thought I had no clue what the fuck he was talking about. He knew a bunch of comics who had just started out and introduced me to them. He also took me to his favorite comedy shows, and I discovered yet another layer to the NYC comedy scene.

It's so crazy because I had no interest in stand-up comedy until I started drinking a lot in New York. I forgot about acting; I never even took one acting class! I think when I got wasted, people would tell me I was hilarious, and I took it very seriously. I thought I was special for being a funny drunk, and I had better make a career out of it. Being an actress wasn't cool enough anymore, I had to do something crazier. That's why I was in a stand-up comedy class preparing to do just that . . . and it was just a few more weeks till my first show.

My hand is so
tired from drawing
pictures just keep
reading ooohkk

Chapter Nine

Our company was slowly falling apart, and people were getting laid off. This Internet business was not easy. It was turning into a feast-or-famine industry, and I knew I was going to get the ax any minute. I wasn't attached to the work itself, but financially it made me nervous to lose another job. The city was expensive, and I *had* to have a decent income. I needed money for rent, food, my first cell phone, cab rides, binge drinking, self-help books, weed, and my new addiction to nicotine. Somewhere along the way, I had become a smoker. It started off with an occasional smoke here and there, and then I discovered that after you put one out you could just light up another one.

Living paycheck to paycheck at an unstable company scared me so much. The thought of not having a job made me nuts, but what was even nuttier was the amount of money I would spend on drinking. One night, I spent $150 on alcohol because I said, "I got this round" a couple of times. It felt good saying that in that moment, but when I woke up the next morning I hated myself for doing that because I needed the money for rent. Besides, I'm a girl. I shouldn't have been spending any money on alcohol. I thought the boys who wanted me to get drunk so I would fool around with them should have bought it. I ended up getting a credit card so I could charge booze and save what I had in my bank account for rent.

Out of the blue, my friend and ex-coworker Reggie, who was a very sassy gay man, e-mailed me and said that he got me an interview at a production company. They were looking for a publicist. When I found out they produced reality TV shows and documentaries and posted videos on the Internet, I wanted the job so bad. Finally, an entertainment job. I thought maybe they'd put me on TV.

A British man, who I could tell lived a sheltered and overprivileged life, interviewed me. I was getting better at sizing people up and judging them right away. My mind was speeding up and my slow, singsongy, small-town girl way of speaking was being replaced with a much faster cadence. I soaked up a lot of PR strategies and lingo that helped me schmooze with executives, and sometimes I felt very professional. I liked saying stuff like "We'll hit the top-tier pubs first, of course, then work our way down to online outlets." New York City had turned me into an overconfident publicist, a self-hating, wannabe stand-up comic, and a drunk.

He offered me the job and shook my hand. He had a weak handshake, which made me happy because it meant I was going to be able to mentally dominate him. I was turning into a psycho! Anyway, it was time to move on. I thanked Liza for everything, sent the cokehead liar boss a nice good-bye e-mail, and left. I don't remember if I gave them two weeks' notice, probably not. The transition was really fast. I was comfortable leaving people, jobs, and situations. I'd get attached for a little bit, but when it was time to go, I was okay with that. I quickly settled into my new cubicle, adjusted to my new workplace neighborhood, Fifth Avenue and Twenty-Fifth Street, and was ready to get everyone at this place to like me.

I'd try to start a casual conversation but these people were very busy and very serious and very unhappy. I didn't like the vibe of this place. I quickly discovered that this company was horrible because the guy who owned it took daily shits on everyone. He had evil pulsing through his veins, and I was his publicist. GROSS. My first job in entertainment dashed my showbiz delusions. I thought it would be so exciting, but it was like this *Wizard of Oz* experience. The exciting and dreamy stuff you see on TV is produced by mean and sad people. I thought if this job couldn't make me happy, I had better become a successful stand-up comic.

The upside in life was comedy class was a-m-a-z-i-n-g. Tommy helped me develop material for my upcoming stand-up comedy show. He said I was the fish-out-of-water type that ended up in crazy situations, and that's good for comedy. I wondered how important it was for a comic to be naturally funny. I also wondered if it was even possible for someone to learn how to be hilarious. That seemed nuts. I thought humor was just something you had or you didn't have, and I was so worried I didn't have it. Sometimes after class I'd pick up a six pack of Corona, go home, drink, chain-smoke, and try to be funny in front of the mirror.

I felt like I was becoming part of the comedy community because I knew I was going to be performing soon. I was more than just a fan; I was a future comic. Stu went with me to shows, and I didn't feel like such a loner. He was the perfect comedy pal. He didn't want to be my boyfriend (turns out he had been married for years and his wife was super, super cool), and he was sort of like me in a way—just wanted to explore comedy and get buzzed. Stu drank, but his drug of choice was weed. He'd carry around a one hitter and would take so many hits from it. It should've been called the million hitter.

During this time I'd fluctuate between being excited and terrified. My mind couldn't decide whether my life was amazing or horrible. I was preparing for my first show and adjusting to my new disappointing entertainment job all at once. I was drinking every night but was very functional. I showed up to work on time, smiled a lot, and only cried in the bathroom. My boss was a nightmare. He had a huge boner for himself and wanted me to get him write-ups in the *New York Times*, the *Washington Post*, and *Wired*. I wanted to be like, "Um, no one cares that you made a show about pet psychics, and I have no idea what your wife sees in you." I soaked up the dark, sad, angry energy in the office. I'd own it and even feel responsible for it. My mom always told me, "You're too sensitive." She was right, but there was nothing I could do it about. I didn't know how to change this about myself. I wish I could have been like, "Hey, mind, body, and soul, reprogram yourself and maybe build an outer robotic shell that deflects dark energy. Thank you so much."

At one point I stopped being afraid of getting fired, because I didn't care. I became combative and less eager to please people at work. I was drinking until 4 a.m. almost every night and was still drunk when I went to work in the morning. By the time the afternoon would roll around, I'd be soooooo tired and worried and shaky and stressed. I started taking more and more cigarette breaks because it was impossible for me to sit at a computer and think of ways to promote that media monger. Our company had a cool roof-top deck and I'd always stand in a spot where no one could see me because I was out there so much. I'd pace and smoke and think about comedy.

, Here I am hiding under an umbrella and smoking and thinking about jumping but only in a just kidding kind of way

My big show was coming up, and the only person I invited was my ex-coworker turned-roommate, Mike. You know the guy from the Magic: The Gathering job who asked me if I passed out under my desk and I said yes, then he let me move into his apartment, and then hooked up the Internet for me? Yeah, him. He and I had become close. We didn't party together anymore, but when we were home we'd always get into these long conversations about life. I think he liked that I was a bit nuts because his background was full of stability, education, and money.

What's the meaning of life

I don't know but remeber the time when you got drunk and brought home a microwave you found in the garbage

I had to work the day of my show and wore the cutest thing I owned, which was black pants and a long-sleeved button-down. I was always amazed that I wasn't a lesbian. I got off work in time to stop and have a drink before my show and prepare my comedy act. I ended up having a few drinks, and it made me feel great. I wrote down my set list on my hand because I didn't want to forget it, even though I'd gone over it about a hundred times in my bedroom the night before. I was going to talk about feeling like a black man in a white lady's body because whenever I walked into an office or room full of people I knew, they were like, "YOOOO TOZER! WUT UP?" and then they'd high-five me. I wasn't sure if this was racist or not, and I just decided it wasn't. I was also going to talk about working in an office and how I wanted to use my eyebrows as Morse code to communicate with coworkers. Like, when I moved my brows up and down I would convey a message like, "The boss is such an asshole. Let's throw him in the East River" or something like that, and I also planned to spit water between my teeth at the audience because I was bad at comedy.

The show was on a Wednesday at 7 p.m. at Stand Up NY, a well-established club on the Upper West Side where professionals performed. I had been to this club before and knew the setup. It wasn't that big; it was a cozy, dark space that smelled like moldy booze and stale barbecue sauce. When I got there I was a little drunk, but it was fine. No one ever really knew when I was drunk, at least I didn't think so. Tommy gave me a hug and told me to stand onstage to see how it felt. I stood up there for a minute looking at the empty seats. I thought about how I was gonna be up there in front of people, and it made me real fuckin' sick.

I went outside to smoke and to really think hard about what I was going to talk about. The audience members slowly began to pour in, including a few black people. I started to second-guess my black man joke. I wanted to ask them if I was a racist. I wanted to tell them I had three black friends and made out with a married black man one time. Mike showed up in a cab, by himself, thank God. I told him not to bring anyone. I told him to go inside because I was busy thinking about everything. Then I thought about how he was a Filipino and one of my good friends, so I was for sure not a racist.

The show was about to start. The host would do ten minutes, then two people from class would perform for the first time, then me. I kept thinking, "Why am I doing this? How did this happen? I wish I could run out the door, get in a cab, go to the airport, and move back in with my grandma Babe." I ordered a vodka tonic and slammed it. I needed more confidence. I was next. Oh shit. I stood where Tommy told me to stand and then I heard something like, "Are you ready for your next comic? She's from Pueblo, Colorado, and this is her first time doing comedy . . . please welcome to the stage . . . Ambbbcrrrr Tooooozzzerrrr." The stage felt like it was a million miles away.

I ran up onstage and felt a burst of energy. I looked out at the audience, and there were only about fifteen people there. I think they were friends of the comics from class, and a few unlucky tourists who got suckered into going to the show. I started talking real fast and loud, just barreling through my jokes. I looked right at the black people when I did my black man bit, ". . . it's like I'm living someone else's stereotype!" Some of them laughed, and some of them didn't. My eyebrow joke got a few laughs, mostly from Tommy and Stu, and the bit where I spit water through my teeth totally bombed. Then it was over. I did it.

Afterward, I felt so relieved. I did it. I did stand-up comedy, something I didn't ever want to do until I moved to New York and became a lush. I wasn't great, but I didn't totally suck ass. Tommy and Stu said I was hilarious, and Mike said I was okay (he was always very honest). I went back and forth from being mad at myself for not being super funny to being happy that at least I did it. All I knew was that I wanted to do it again. Tommy said he'd get me on another show soon.

Going back to the office the next day felt so stupid and pointless. I thought, "Look at these idiots, working for the Man. These people are sheep." It's like I became an instant self-righteous artist who judged everyone who didn't live their dreams.

What a snobby artist sees when they look at people who work for the Man

ew

Nikki and I had grown apart, but every once in a while we'd get shitfaced together. Sometimes we'd go to this bar called Rodeo. I loved it. It was a Tex Mex restaurant that had a backspace where bands would perform, and they had the best happy-hour margarita specials. These drinks were incredible; they were nicknamed *liquid crack*. I loved them so much it made me want to try crack. Two of these margaritas would make me feel like I was a god, a god of feeling really fucking fantastic and I thought Nikki felt the same way. I guess I was wrong because one day she invited me out to lunch and told me she was going to rehab. She explained that she had been doing too much coke and just needed a break from partying. I told her that I didn't know she had a problem, and she said she hid it from a lot of people. I said okay and kept eating my salad. I could tell she was looking for a bigger reaction out of me, probably because I had been binge drinking with her for the past year and I was her friend. I should've been concerned or more supportive. But I honestly didn't think much about it because I was buried so deep in self-obsession that anything that didn't revolve around me didn't mean much. I thought it was good she was going to rehab; coke was bad news. But at the same time, I didn't want to get too involved because I didn't have a drug problem. I just liked to "party."

We stopped hanging out after this happened, and it didn't phase me. When you're drunk all of the time, you don't care about anyone but yourself and all you want to do is feel good and escape discomfort. Helping other people, or even caring about them too much, isn't possible. It either felt like an inconvenience or a situation that needed intimacy and empathy. No, thank you.

My routine continued and I was very busy with work and comedy, but inside I felt rotten, like something was horribly wrong. I had developed self-hatred, self-pity, and a taste for self-destruction. Depression, anxiety, and paranoia began to rule every thought I had and every choice I made. My head was very loud during this time. It felt like there was a group of mean people living in my head, people who encouraged me to do bad things, and another group of people who convinced me to hate myself for doing those bad things. There was a hellish war going on in my mind, and I was an active participant on both sides of it. Thank God for comedy. Sure, it was a bad environment for me because it encouraged drinking, but it was also a saving grace because it gave me something creative and challenging to focus on. Comedy inspired me to work hard. Being involved with it made me feel like I was doing "something."

Tommy finally booked me on that second show he promised me, and I worked my ass off on writing new jokes. It was another weeknight show. I invited this guy Sam from work to go with me. He was a producer and was one of the few people at work who didn't seem suicidal. On our way to the gig, we stopped and had two of those liquid crack margaritas, and I got pretty tanked. The show was at Don't Tell Mama, a piano bar in Midtown. It was packed. Mike, Liza, Al, and a few other friends showed up. I decided to invite friends because I was sick of hiding my secret love of comedy. Stu, of course, was there baked like, "Hey, man, are you ready to rock or what?" I was drunk, so yes, I was ready to rock. When it was my turn to hit the stage, I let it fuckin' rip. I talked about real things that happened to me and playing basketball and my family. The material was more personal. I felt connected to it, and I killed.

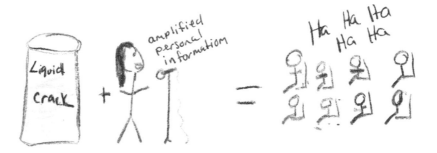

I was hooked. My obsession with comedy escalated, and I wanted to perform all of the time. If I wasn't on a show, I was watching a show. I thought since performing was the only thing that made me happy (besides being drunk), it must mean that this was what I was supposed to do with my life. I was still afraid of the cool alternative scene, but all I had to do was get real fucking sloshed before I went to a show and everything was fine. One of my goals was to get on a Monday night show called "Eating It." It was at Luna Lounge, a rock club in the East Village that occasionally hosted comedy events. The show's producer, Jeff, would always book one or two new comics and it was a BIG DEAL. It was a hot shit show because comics like Sarah Silverman, Janeane Garofalo, Patton Oswalt, Tig Notaro, Todd Barry, Marc Maron, and Bill Burr would perform. I wanted to get on that show so bad, and I was there every Monday night slamming drinks, chain-smoking, and talking to my comedy heroes and trying to get Jeff to like me.

One morning after a night of partying at Luna, I took the 2, 3 red line train to work like I always did. I was tired and hungover and not looking forward to sitting at my desk all day counting down the hours until it was time to leave. As I was exiting the train station at Twenty-Third and Seventh Avenue, I saw a really tall, muscular man crying on his cell phone in the stairwell. I thought, "Wow, a tough guy crying. You don't see that every day." Then I walked out onto the sidewalk and the city was silent. It was the craziest thing. I felt like I had just entered some slow-motion alternative universe. Everyone was standing still and staring downtown. I walked over to Sixth Avenue and asked a man in a suit what was going on. He pointed and said,

Chapter Ten

I looked down Sixth Avenue and had a clear view of a gaping, burning hole in the South Tower. This is when I left my body and did not return to it for a while.

I stood there with the man in the suit for a minute, both of us just watching it burn. A lot of people were on their phones, their free hand waving around as they explained to their loved ones what was happening. Everyone else looked like well-dressed zombies.

After The First Plane Hit

The World Trade Center is on fire

I'm ok dad

A plane flew right into it

I think we should break up life is too short to play games

I ran the remaining two blocks to my office building, my heart pounding as I rode the elevator to the seventh floor. When I got to the office, there were a handful of people in the conference room, mostly producers and executives, their eyes were glued to the TV. "A plane just hit the second tower" someone said to me as I walked in to stare at the TV. I was like, "OH MY FUCKING GOD, ARE YOU SERIOUS" as if someone would joke about that.

I called the Do Drop Inn to talk to my mom, but she wasn't there and she didn't have a cell phone. I told the waitress who answered to tell my mom I was okay, and I would call her later. A few more people straggled into work and a group of us went out to the rooftop deck to see what was going on in the streets. There were thousands, maybe millions of people walking somewhere. Were they going home or to a friend's house or to check on their family? I didn't know. I lit up a cigarette and stared at all of the skyscrapers. The weather was beautiful, a clear blue sky that turned to fire at the southern tip of Manhattan.

A loud roar came from the people in the conference room. They were reacting to the plane that just hit the Pentagon. "Jesus Fucking Christ," I said. Everyone in the office was on the phone calling their families. I called my mom again at the Do Drop, and she was there. "Mom, I'm okay." She said, "Okay. Good. Where are you?" I told her I was at work and would have to stay there because the trains weren't working but I'd be okay. She told me to be careful, and I was like, "Uh. Okay." How can you be careful when planes are slamming into buildings? I'd always get mad at Mom for acting like a mom, even during a terrorist attack.

The executives were pacing and talking quietly to each other, then everyone was called into one area and they announced that they were going to shoot a documentary at Ground Zero. A few cameramen were there, along with a few producers and me. One of the execs asked if I wanted to go down to the towers with a cameraman and get some interviews from people on the street. Without thinking about it I said, "Yes, I'll go." A few minutes later, I was walking down Fifth Avenue with a group of cameramen and producers, on our way to the towers.

After a few minutes of walking, we decided to split up into groups of two or three. I teamed up with a guy who I didn't know that well, a freelancer who I had seen in the office a few times. He had a big camera on his shoulder, and we started walking together. I was going back and forth in my mind about what was happening. I didn't want to bother anyone. Everyone looked so miserable and freaked out, and I felt like we were capitalizing on this tragedy. Then I thought about all of the other documentaries on wars and tragic events and how educational they are and how important it is to document history. I convinced myself what we were doing was important and was going to be useful in the future, so I decided to just keep going. I wasn't afraid of dying; I was afraid of bothering people.

We took a right at some point and headed west. We were about two or three miles north of the towers, and this is when everyone in the streets let out a collective "AHHHHHH." I didn't know what happened, what happened?? We ran over to Sixth Avenue, and there was a huge cloud of smoke and debris bellowing up from the ground where the first tower once stood, it had just collapsed. Another, "Jesus Fucking Christ" came out of my mouth. I couldn't believe it. We were far enough away to not feel like we were in harm's way, but at the same time I thought about more attacks, more planes hitting. I kept looking up to see if there were any more planes.

More and more people started to head uptown as we continued downtown. People were gathered in groups on street corners, listening to homeless people's radios. New York is diverse no doubt, but it was rare to see businessmen, cabbies, hippies, sophisticated women, construction workers, and homeless people all huddling together around a battery-operated boom box that was blasting the news.

The second tower came crashing down. This is when I thought I might die, not because we were close to the towers (we were still about a mile away) but because something like this was really happening. I mean, if planes could crash into the World Trade Center, and then the towers came crashing down, why couldn't I just die for no reason? I had this overwhelming feeling that whatever I thought life was about, or whatever I thought I knew about anything, wasn't real. And I thought about how much of life is out of our control. I had never had that thought before.

We kept heading downtown. I wondered about the people who just died. What did they do the night before? Did they hug their families this morning? I wondered what in the hell you would do if you were in one of those buildings. What about the people who were late to work or called in sick today? I wondered if I knew anyone who worked at the WTC. I didn't. I thought about how the WTC was my train stop when I worked "down on Wall Street." I wondered if the bar I used to get shitfaced at was covered in debris. My mind was going nuts. We needed to take a break from walking, and the cameraman said we should go somewhere we could get some interviews. We went to a bar.

It was packed in there. I wanted a beer so bad but didn't want the cameraman to see me drink. The thought of getting wasted was so tempting and so terrifying. I didn't want to ask people for an interview but I did. I started asking people what they saw and if they knew anyone who worked at the WTC, and if they wanted to be interviewed. Some people did; some people didn't. If a person agreed to talk, we would prompt them with a question and record whatever they said. Most people talked about where they were when it happened and how they felt. It was awful. I knew that if I was drunk, it would be easier for me to talk to these people. I was so thirsty and hungry, but I didn't feel hungover anymore. I guess a good cure for a hangover is being in the middle of a terrorist attack.

After we got a few interviews, we walked farther downtown and ended up at a park. I think it was the one in front of City Hall. I don't remember. We weren't allowed to go any farther. There were police barricades and medical kiosks set up everywhere. There was about an inch of debris from the towers on the ground; paperwork from financial institutions was scattered everywhere. I picked up a piece of paper that had letterhead from J.P. Morgan, and then I picked up a pair of broken glasses. I thought, "Whose glasses are these? Was it someone who was in the building? Or was it someone who was safe at home who had just left their glasses at work?" My thoughts raced. There was a large group of people making stretchers out of wood planks for people injured in the attack. The cameraman started filming them, and a few people got pissed off. They yelled, "Stop filming and start helping us!" A police officer said quietly, "There aren't going to be any bodies. Anyone who didn't make it out of those buildings before they collapsed is gone."

We filmed for a few more hours, got a couple more interviews, and made our way back to the office. I just wanted to go home, but there was no way to get to Brooklyn. The trains were shut down. Sam invited me to stay at his place. He lived uptown somewhere; I forget where exactly. We left the office that afternoon and planned to go back to work the next day. Sam and I made it back to his place and drank whiskey. I hated whiskey, but I drank it.

I was happy to be with him because he was such a positive person, but when I was ready to go to bed, he hit on me. I was like, "DUDE, COME ON I AM WEAK AND VULNERABLE AND IN SHOCK AND DRUNK BUT NOT DESPERATE." He backed off right away. We laughed about it, but I was still sort of pissed. Then I thought about bonin' him because maybe the next day bombs would be falling from the sky. It'd be sort of beautiful to have sex knowing you were gonna die in a few hours. But as much as I drank, I didn't sleep with guys who I didn't love. Sure, I'd make out with them (I'd make out with anyone). I'd blue-ball them, and let them touch my tiny boobs, but sex was too intense for me. Most guys disgusted me, even if they were cute. The only men that I was attracted to were the types that could ruin my life, the unavailable fucked-up guys. I liked having sex with guys who had a lot of problems because it was exciting. It was a challenge to try to change them, and I liked focusing on other people's problems rather than my own. Sam was a good guy. He was slightly dorky with a stable job—not my type, not even on 9/11.

I slept in his roommate's room and had sex with his roommate. Just kidding—his roommate wasn't home. The next morning was awkward, but the intensity of the terrorist attacks outweighed any silly, flirty drama. We both went to the office. I was in the same clothes; I smelled like whiskey. I didn't know what to do with myself. They needed people to transcribe footage from the day before, people to watch and type up every single word that was said on film. So that's what I did. I watched hours and hours of footage from the streets on 9/11 and typed up the sad stories they told. I listened to countless interviews of New Yorkers giving their take on what happened, and it was fucking up my mind. Some people were matter of fact about it; some people were emotional; some people were like robots. I had to stop. I wanted to go home.

I stayed at work until the sun went down, then walked all the way downtown by myself. The streets were littered with pictures of missing people. I looked at some of their faces and thought about what they were thinking when the planes hit. Can you fucking imagine? I got as close as I could to Ground Zero, sneaking past a few areas blocked off by police tape. I sat on a stoop and watched bulldozers work under the lights. It was unfucking real. It was this massive pile of debris, no way could they clean that up. No way.

I thought about where I was on the morning of September 11. I was on the red 2, 3 line that went directly under the World Trade Center. I thought, "Maybe I was right under it when the first plane hit at 8:45 a.m." Then I thought, "Who gives a shit. Quit trying to make this a dramatic story about you. You aren't dead and a lot of people are fucking dead, right there in that pile of debris in front of you." I don't remember how I made it home that night but I did. Maybe it was the green 4, 5 line or maybe it was a cab. I took the next day off from work.

The next month was a blur. I was drinking a lot. Work was nonstop 9/11 footage, and comedy was awkward. I didn't perform for a while and was in awe of comics who were talking about the attacks. I'd go to shows, get wasted, and listen to how the professionals were handling such a huge event like this. They riffed on Bin Laden, Bush, and gave personal accounts of where they were when it happened and made it funny. No way could I do that. What would I say? "I helped make a movie about it! I was running around begging people to talk about it on camera—the more tragic their story, the better!" I just drank and watched.

I couldn't find anything funny about this

The people of New York during this time were incredible. Everyone was nicer and a little slower and more present. It was like everyone went through an empathy class, and we were all just real fucking cool to each other. We were on the same team, and the spirit of the city rallied and made a comeback. Before long, we were all being assholes to each other again, and it was great.

Hello   Have a good day   September 12th

Hey there   Good afternoon   September 13th

Hi   Go fuck yourself   September 14th

Just when the city started to feel normal again, I quit my job. I couldn't take it anymore. That company was a hellhole before it wrapped its claws around the 9/11 material, and after that it morphed into a hellhole that created other hellholes. It was like a breeding ground for hellholes, and I had to escape. I didn't have another gig lined up, so I asked the finance guy, "If I quit, can I get unemployment?" He told me to file, and he'd take care of it. BOOM. I got unenjoy-ment and started performing and writing jokes again and going out every single night. Maybe I'd take one night off here and there, but I couldn't stand being home alone.

Drinking had turned into a beast of a necessity, not only for social situations but for any situation. If I was home on the weekend and wanted to clean my room, I'd have to have a couple of drinks before I could focus on picking up dirty laundry. And at night—forget about it. I'd try to control it but then forgot that I was trying to control it and just got hammered. I'd black out a couple of times a week. Blackouts are amazing. You are doing stuff for hours, then you pass out, and then when you wake up, you have no idea what you did during those hours. Some people get in fights, some people take a bus to Atlantic City and have a great time, and some people, like me, talk to strangers for hours, then get in a cab and go home. I somehow always made it back home safely, so other than having a brutal hangover, the consequences weren't that bad.

One night, I got really wasted at the comedy show at Luna Lounge. Well, I got wasted there, and then I got even more wasted at a bar down the street after the show. Then I caught a cab home. The next thing I remember, I am lying down in the back of a cab slobbering on the seat. I popped up and had no idea where I was. I looked at the meter, and it was almost fifty bucks. It usually only cost me $12 to get home at that time of night. I started yelling at the cab driver, "Hey! Where the fuck are we?" He said, "I've been yelling at you to wake up for 30 minutes! I'm lost! This is my first night driving!" I redirected him best I could, and we eventually made it back to my place. The entire time I was yelling, "Turn off the meter! I'm not paying you fifty dollars! No way! You got lost, man."

He kept arguing that it was my fault for falling asleep. I didn't even have fifty bucks! He stopped in front of my apartment building on Eastern Parkway and Classon. I threw a twenty-dollar bill through the glass window that separated the front seat from the back. Then I got out of the cab and started to walk away; he walked after me. I noticed my cell phone wasn't in my pocket. FUCK. I said, "Okay, I'll give you more money" and walked back to the cab. There was my cell phone, in the backseat. I opened the door, grabbed it, then started running. I wasn't gonna give him any more money. I just wanted my cell phone, sucker! He started chasing after me. Holy fucking shit. I started sprinting and tried to channel my old college athlete days. I could not believe he was actually running after me. He left the cab in the middle of the street!

I rounded a corner and saw two really big black guys leaning up against a car. I was like, "Hey, there is a man chasing me. Can you help me?" They said, "Yeah, where's he at?" Sure enough the cabbie came huffing and puffing around the corner, and the big guys were like, "Yo. What the fuck's your problem?" The cabbie tried to explain that I owed him money, but I started screaming over him, "Leave me alone, you psycho!" He just stood there, defeated. He wasn't going to win; he turned around and walked away. I thanked the guys, and we immediately hit it off. They were so cool and chatty and nice. I was still very drunk, but not blacked-out and very aware and wanted to hang out with these guys. They asked, "Soo . . . do you smoke weed?" I said, "Absolutely!" Then I got in their car. They said they were about to go pick up some shwag from a friend.

We drove to a deli somewhere in Brooklyn, one of those corner delis where you could buy a hammer, a roll of toilet paper, and a turkey sandwich. I loved those one-stop bodegas; they're like a combination of a hardware store and a grocery store. They said the cashier was their friend and would sell us weed. After we purchased the goods we proceeded to get super, super, super high and just drove around Brooklyn. One guy was a truck driver, and the other guy was a chef. They lived in my neighborhood. We talked about the big picture of life, like what was really important and what the meaning of everything was. They both agreed that it was all about love. I was like, "Yeah, man."

The sun started to come up, and I told them I had better get home. My booze buzz was wearing off. I was exhausted and my awareness of riding around with two strangers after getting chased by a cabbie started to sink in. We exchanged phone numbers and hugs and promised to keep in touch. As I walked into my apartment, I had mixed feelings about what just happened. On one hand, I thought, "What a fun adventure! I'm so adventurous!" and on the other, "That was stupid. You're insane." I didn't know which thought to believe and went to bed.

I woke up thinking the second thought, "You're an idiot." I was so mortified that I had yelled at the cabbie, run away from him, then duped two men into scaring him, then willingly hopped in their backseat and went cruising for weed. Sure, it was fun and those guys were all about love, but still. I felt like a couple years ago I would have laughed so hard at what happened, but my drinking was starting to scare me. My behavior wasn't funny anymore, and my hangovers were full of regret, even if I had a fun time the night before. I knew something was wrong with the way I drank. I just couldn't wrap my head around it. I told Mike what happened, his innocent eyes wide as he listened to me tell the story. He said, "Bear," that was his nickname for me, "You're fuckin' nuts." He was right.

THE MORNING AFTER

I can't believe I did that

"You can't even let your old man know you're in town doing a show?" my dad said as he held up the article about me in the Pueblo newspaper. I was home for the holidays, and my mom let me do a big comedy show at the Do Drop Inn. I had been performing for almost two years now and was ready to tell my jokes in front of everyone in my hometown. My mom had opened up a second Do Drop Inn location. It was huge. It could seat almost 200 people, and we packed it out! I was so happy because we charged a few bucks at the door, and I got to keep all of the money. I invited friends and family, and the paper wrote about it. I didn't invite my dad because I didn't want to. He was a man who I didn't like and saw twice a year out of guilt. I told him I was sorry. I wasn't sorry. I wanted to say, "Why didn't I invite you? Oh, I don't know. Maybe it's the same reason why you're a shitty father. We're both shitty people!"

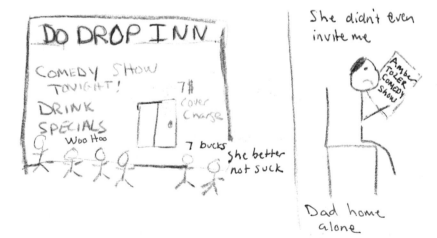

His life, his attitude, and his health were getting worse. He had moved into a shoebox-size studio apartment in an old apartment building that seemed like it was built specifically for old men who regretted their choices in life. My dad had a small, old TV with an antenna, a bunch of weird knicknacks you'd buy at a flea market, pictures of us kids everywhere, and a futon Adam bought him because he was sleeping on the floor. I saw a bottle of vodka on the top of his refrigerator and wondered how much he drank.

My dad was a master at hiding his alcoholism from us; he was a closet drinker. I had only seen him intoxicated once in my life. It was when I stopped by unannounced when I was in college; I could smell it on him. I was like, "Are you drunk?" He said he had been drinking whiskey because his back hurt. My mom once told me that my grandpa Tozer was a drunk (making that two drunk grandpas), and my dad was terrified of being an alcoholic, so he hid it and tried to control his drinking. He'd go on benders, then stop for a while. I think his shame around alcohol inspired some control, some sober phases, but this didn't help because his mental health was deteriorating fast. He ended up in the hospital a few times because he thought he was having a heart attack. I just thought he was being dramatic and was doing it for attention. I hated him. I thought I was ripped off as a kid for having such a negative, whiny loser dad. I felt so awful after spending time with him. It was a mix of hatred and guilt for hating him. I was too mad at him to feel sorry for him.

My relationship with the rest of my family felt far away. The distance between Pueblo and NYC was equivalent to the emotional distance that had grown between us. They were all very cool and welcoming and nice to me, but I had morphed into an entirely different person, while they all stayed the same. I was on the outside of a tribe that I used to be in the middle of. I don't know if they noticed this because I was physically there, smiling and being like, "Hello, how are you doing? Yeah, comedy is going great. I love New York." I acted like a civilized human, but on the inside I felt completely nuts. Maybe it was 9/11, or because I was always hungover, or maybe it was because I had left their world and entered a place so foreign that it changed my entire psychological makeup.

Partying in a big city and experimenting with new jobs and challenges and being overexposed to everything, from culture and art and business to parties on skyscraper rooftops and smoking pot in grungy dance club basements completely changed me. It was like I had taken a trip to another planet, and aliens cracked open my mind and inserted new grooves in my brain, programming me to operate and perceive life in an entirely new way. It was very difficult for me to relate to my family when I was home. I was a new person. In some ways it was good; I loved transforming and growing. But at this point, I was very selfish and self-destructive and put my needs before everyone else's.

I loved my sisters, Autumn and Rochelle, very much, but I thought since they were so young and hadn't experienced much outside of Pueblo, I wouldn't be able to connect with them. I didn't even think to call them to see how *they* were doing. I thought since they didn't have much to offer me, I gave them the bare bones of what I could give. Adam and I were cool with each other. We'd hang and drink together, and he'd let me crash at his place. But he had started his own business and was very busy. Once I was back in NYC, we were out of touch. My mom and I got along, but there was so much I didn't want to tell her about my life because she'd be mortified. I'm pretty sure she didn't want to know. I think as long as I was alive my mom was okay with whatever I didn't tell her. Plus, she had a lot to deal with. The new Do Drop location was all-consuming; she had a new boyfriend; Rochelle had been diagnosed with type 1 diabetes. It was such a scary nightmare: insulin shots at 4 a.m., checking her blood sugar, changing her diet, doctors appointments, etc.

Rochelle had the worst luck. I didn't mention this earlier in the book because I had to blast through my early years, so I could get to the real dark and dirty NYC stuff, but Rochelle's hair fell out when she was four. Right before the car accident, she developed alopecia, a hair-loss virus, and lost ALL OF HER HAIR. So not only did this little girl lose her hair and survive a deadly car accident, she now had to take three shots a day and monitor her blood sugar levels so she didn't slip into a coma. My mom was stressed out about this, so I didn't feel comfortable telling her, "Hey, Mom. I'm binge drinking seven nights a week and day jobs make me suicidal, but the good news is, I love telling dick jokes. Sorry about Rochelle."

My mom was strong and smart, but sometimes she felt unavailable and wasn't the best fit for me to hash things out with. She's not emotional and prefers practicality and common sense over everything, whereas I love to overanalyze human behavior and talk about feelings and am always twisting things up in my mind, then detangling them. She's like, "Let's go. Move it. Move on." Or she'd start giving me advice before I could finish a sentence. So it got to the point where I wouldn't open up to her because I already knew what her response would be. Plus, she never really told me about what was going on in her life.

Mom: How are you doing
Me: Fine How are you
Mom: Good

The End

Oh God, one time when I was back home visiting for Christmas, I got SO MAD at her. It was Christmas Eve and I was hungover. I had stayed with her the night before, I don't remember where I got drunk, but I was in bad shape that morning. I ran to Walmart in my pajamas, like everyone who goes to Walmart does, and did some last-minute white-trash Christmas shopping. When I got back to her house, she was dressed up real fancy. I was like, "Are you going to Church?" She said, "Um. No. Wayne and I are getting married." I said, "WHAT? WHERE?" She said, "In the living room."

Wayne was her farmer boyfriend who she had been dating for a while. He was a nice guy, but I didn't know him that well. All I knew was that he didn't drink a lot because my grandma said, "Well, at least this one is not an alcoholic." I didn't care if he was the president of Pueblo, I was so pissed. I yelled, "DID YOU TELL ANYONE ABOUT THIS?" My mom said she didn't want to make a big deal about it because she had been married before and just wanted to get it over with. A marriage is a huge deal whether your wedding is on top of Mount Everest and you're surrounded by whoever didn't die on the way to the top or in a recently vacuumed living room with your closest friends like it's a surprise party. A few minutes later, Wayne, his best friend, my mom's best friend, and a priest showed up. There I was, hungover in my pajamas, watching my mom get married to a farmer I had met a few times. Wayne was like, "I'm glad you're here, kid! You can take pictures!" and handed me a disposable camera. I took a picture of our dog, Jake, then stormed upstairs. I thought, "A sophisticated New York family would never do something like this."

The Only Picture I took at my Mom's Wedding

OUR DOG JAKE'S BODY

Everyone in the family was upset about this. We were at my aunt Sabrina's house for our traditional Christmas Eve party giving my mom shit. "We can't believe you didn't invite us!" My grandma Babe was like, "What in the hell is the matter with you people?" Me, Autumn, Rochelle, and Adam gave her the silent treatment all night. Later, around midnight, Adam and I got stoned in her driveway and made a plan to teepee her house. I snuck in there to get toilet paper, but there weren't enough rolls in the guest bathroom. Luckily, my mom's best friend from high school, a hilarious hippie named Janice, always bought everyone in our family a roll of paper towels for Christmas. So, there was about twenty rolls of paper towels under the tree. I grabbed a few of 'em and ran back outside. Then me and Adam, buzzed and stoned out of our minds, paper-toweled our own mother's house on Christmas Eve because she got married in the living room and didn't invite us.

Welcome To The FAMILY
WAYNE

At least the dysfunctional family stuff was great for comedy. I told this story onstage and everyone asked, "Did that really happen?" YES, IT HAPPENED! My mom got me a new dad for Christmas! I loved being able to turn stuff that made me mad into comedy. I didn't think I was that great at coming up with hard hitting punch lines, but I was good at developing weird little left-of-center bits and telling stories. I was onstage six nights a week, constantly thinking of new ideas, and was now fully immersed in the alternative scene. I knew a few semifamous comics who told me I was funny, and it both inflated my ego and made me nervous. It put the pressure of "You have to be great all the time now" on me.

I finally got booked on "Eating It" at Luna Lounge. I was soooo fucking nervous, but it ended up going really well. I did this bit where I held up a tape recorder and played a recording of myself singing "Stay" by Lisa Loeb. I sounded real crazy in it, like a drunk girl singing karaoke. I set it up like this, "I called my ex-boyfriend to let him know that I missed him. Here's a recording of the call." Then I held up the tape recorder to the microphone and mouthed the words real dramatically, closing my eyes and getting emotional. I got drunk before I went onstage, and got wasted after I got off. Whether I had a good show or a bad show, I drank a lot.

Drinking was an absolute necessity for me at this point, and the comedy world enabled me beautifully. Comics rarely get paid to do comedy, but we almost always get free drinks. I was extra nice to the bartenders. So after I drank my two free drinks, they'd give me more free drinks. Then I'd flirt with boys, so they would buy me drinks. I loved not spending money on booze; there was no way I could afford it. I was still on unemployment but had gotten a part-time gig that paid under the table. I was an assistant to a crazy lady, Katie, who let me chain-smoke and drink in the office. She worked in TV and film distribution, and she just needed help around the office.

Katie was hilarious and wild and more dysfunctional than I was; we became twisted sisters of sorts. She took me to France with her one time for a conference. I got so drunk I made out with a guy from New Jersey. I woke up the next morning mad at myself because I was in France and made out with a Jersey boy. I had bought into the whole "Jersey is the armpit of America" joke that people on the East Coast say. I was like, "I kissed a boy from JERSEY while I'm in FRANCE? Oy." I had also picked up some stereotypical Jewish traits. Oh, and Katie got so tanked that night she brought a guy back to our hotel room, and I stayed in the bathroom and flossed until they were finished fooling around.

Vive la France

One day, back in New York, Katie told me to make sure the office looked nice because she was meeting with a bigwig producer from L.A. I Googled him and saw all of the shows he had produced and thought, "Wow. This guy is big. Maybe if he likes me, he'll change my life." After their meeting he was walking to the elevator, and I slowly crept up behind him. I got in the elevator with him and told him I just needed some fresh air. Then, I not so casually mentioned that I did stand-up comedy. He got really excited and said that's how he started out, writing jokes for comics. He was so cool! We ended up talking for a while, then he gave me his card, and told me to keep in touch. He wanted to see a tape of my comedy. WHOA.

I was working a few days a week for Katie, and the rest of the time it was comedy, comedy, comedy. Stu introduced me to more comics. One of his best friends was this guy Andy. He made a living doing shows on the road and corporate gigs, and I just thought that was incredible. I met Jen, a tough, skinny, Irish girl from Philly who did a joke about how there should be an ashtray built into strollers for edgy moms. I was like, "Holy shit, that girl is smart. She should be a businesswoman." And another comic I met was Stacey, a lesbian whose main goal in life was to be super cool. She worked at a bank and ran a show every Tuesday night at a dive bar in Chinatown, which was right next to a meat market that had dead chickens in the window. I loved this all so much.

Stu, Andy, and I went to a lot of shows together. If Andy had a spot somewhere, we'd go and support him and then go to another show somewhere just to watch. We were always smoking pot and drinking, but nothing too crazy. I was up for anything new and said yes to a lot of random stuff, and that's how I ended up in a comedy punk rock band called Happy Ending with these guys. Remember my comedy teacher, Tommy? Well, he was doing a show every Saturday night and wanted a band to play a theme song, so we became his band. Stu played the guitar, Andy played the drums and was lead vocals, and I pretended to play the bass and let my hair fall in my face.

Stu wrote a few original songs, and before I knew it, we were our own musical-comedy act performing at clubs all over the city. I never really learned how to play the bass because I didn't want to, and we were horrible. We had one funny song called "Things I Would Rather Do." I sang it really loud like a rocker chick. It was about me meeting a boy on a bus who wanted to have sex with me, but I thought he was gross, and would rather do horrible things than have sex with him. Our time as a band was short-lived because at one point we were all like, "What the fuck are we doing?"

Our Hit Song
"Sex With You"

Doing my taxes missing my plane
Watching my house go up in flames
These are the things I would
rather do than have sex with you

Chewin on tin foil
Bein sprayed with mace
gettin kicked in the fuckin face
These are the things I'd
rather do than have sex
with you

I'm not that kind of girl and even if I was
I wouldn't screw a loser like you that I just
met on the bus

Jen, the skinny tough girl from Philly, turned into an older-sister type. She wasn't into the party scene; she had a serious boyfriend, Marc, and they both had their shit together. They'd always have me over for dinner, and Jen would tell me to be careful after I told her one of my stories. Jen drank wine and smoked cigarettes, but it was in a sophisticated French sort of way. Stacey was a big drinker. When she wasn't working on being cool, she'd party pretty hard with me. We'd get wasted all of the time and one time we made out. I was taking my tomboyishness to the next level—bisexual activity. I had made out with a few girls before when I was drunk, so it wasn't a big deal. I was like, "Hey, are you a human? Okay, great. Let's get sexy together."

You better be careful girls

Jen

When I'm done being cool I am going to kiss you Amber

Stacey

ok I should be drunk enough by then

I was always mortified the morning after making out with girls and strangers I met on the street. But I had gotten to a place with my drinking where I was drunk all of the time, so I only spent a few hours being riddled with shame before I was drunk again. My life had become one long, drunken comedy show followed up with a horrible hangover. It's just how it was. I found a way to use comedy as a way to binge drink and chain-smoke. I romanticized it, like I was some sort of interesting and troubled movie character in an independent film about stand-up comedy in the early 2000s. The truth was that I was just a drunk who had to drink.

One morning, hungover and thirsty, I got out of bed to get some water and I couldn't open my bedroom door. The building we lived in was pretty old, so our doors were all fucked-up and wouldn't close and open sometimes. We never did anything about it because we never paid attention to what our apartment looked like. I had been sleeping on a futon for years and had a life-size Batman poster on the wall. I wasn't even that into Batman, but I thought I should put something on the wall. Mike had a nice bed, but you couldn't even see his floor because it was covered in dirty clothes and comic books. Al was sort of a pig, too. Anyway, I was locked in my bedroom. I tried so hard to get that door open but couldn't. Mike had already left for work, and I was home alone. He said he couldn't make it back right away but would come back in a few hours. I thought maybe I could just go back to bed or keep myself busy until he got back, but I eventually had to pee.

I held it for as long as I could before I had to surrender to the fact that I was going to have to pee in my bedroom. I started to look for a good spot. The closet? Maybe, but my shoes were in there. A Diet Coke can? No, I'd probably pee all over my hand. Hmmm . . . I scanned the room and saw a plastic bag on the floor. I thought, "Perfect! I'll pee in that bag!" I grabbed it, pulled down my pajama pants, straddled the bag, and just let it go. The bag was sturdy and I felt confident it wouldn't break, but I thought maybe it would overflow. It was one of those pees where you're amazed at your bladder for holding that much liquid. It just felt good to be releasing it. I caught a glimpse of myself in the mirror and sort of tried to look sexy for minute, and then I was like, "What are you doing, you weirdo?"

This is the fifth pee story in this book so far do you think I am gonna win a Pulitzer or what

That brief moment of bliss ended when I had to figure out what to do with the bag. It was so full, and the pee was sloshing around. One little slip and my room would be doused in boozy urine. Ugh. I thought, "Wait a minute, the window! It didn't have a screen on it, and there is a little ledge! I'll just put it out there!" The window in my bedroom overlooked a courtyard. Well, I think *courtyard* is too fancy of a word to use. There was a big patch of grass, and sometimes I'd see people out there with their dogs. Anyway, I put the bag, which I noticed was a Chinese delivery bag with a receipt stapled to the side, on the ledge and shut the window. Then, as I was pulling up my pants, I heard a crinkle sound and a *thud*. I looked out the window and the bag had fallen over the ledge. I thought, "Shit, my name and address are on the receipt of that Chinese delivery bag! People are gonna know it's me!"

Oh great now humans
are peeing in the court
yard

Evidence

sniff
sniff

Mike eventually came back home and was able to get me out. Or maybe it was Al, I don't remember. (The hard part about writing a memoir about being a drunk is being able to remember things. As I've been writing this I'm like, "Did that happen in 2003 or 2005?" And, "Was that guy's name Chris or Charlie or was he a woman?") Anyways, Mike or Al got me out of that fucking bedroom and I was worried that someone in the building might find out it was me. I thought about going to the dogshit courtyard and throwing the bag away, but I didn't want to do deal with it. The next morning I looked over the ledge, and the pee bag was gone. Good job, maintenance cleanup!

Where did the bag
of pee go

If you pet me
for an hour I
will tell you

I ended up telling the pee-bag story onstage, and it turned out to be my best bit. I embellished the ending by saying, ". . . and everyone found out it was me because the bag I peed in was a Chinese delivery bag with the receipt stapled to the side. It had my name, my address, my lunch order. Now when I walk into the building people say, 'There she is, she lives in apartment 3C, she likes chicken and broccoli, and she drops urine bombs. She's fuckin' crazy.'" It was my favorite joke for a long time, and it worked in both mainstream and alternative rooms. A timeless joke for all to enjoy.

Occasionally Andy, Stu, and I would go to a popular open mic called "The Bad Accident." If you wanted to perform, you'd put your name in a bucket and wait for one of the hosts to call your name. You could go up first or fiftieth. It was a nightmare. The show was run by these two New York comics, Darren and Vinnie. They were both real smart and confident and everyone knew who they were. Darren talked about how dumb everyone was, and Vinnie had a real thick Brooklyn accent and would yell a lot. Vinnie was angry and loud and honest. I told Andy I thought he was so cute.

One day, while I was at work, Vinnie called and said in his real thick Brooklyn accent, "Hey, how ya doin? I got your numbah from Andy. Why don't you stop by 'The Bad Accident' tonight and I'll give ya a ride home after the show?" I said, "Um, okay. See you later." I loved how direct he was. He got straight to the fuckin' point. Meet me here. I'll take you home. One of the reasons I hated dating so much is because there's so much bullshit wondering if the other person wants to spend time with you. I loved that Vinnie just told me to meet him. He didn't ask. Sexy.

I showed up later in the night because that show would go on until two in the morning. I didn't want to sit there for hours waiting for Vinnie to be done with his show, not because it would be boring, but because I didn't want him to know that I liked him enough to sit through a four-hour open mic. I arrived casually late, had a few drinks, and waited for him. I got drunk, but not super drunk. My tolerance was so high for alcohol, I could have four or five drinks and act somewhat normal. He drove me back to my place, and I invited him in. I was nervous because my place was messy. I didn't know I'd have a boy over that night. I suggested we stay in the living room because I didn't have TV in my room. Plus, my room was a disaster. I didn't have cable. All I had was a VHS/DVD combo player and was like, "Here we can watch this," and put in an old tape of me playing high school basketball.

It was so ridiculous. We were sitting on my old crappy couch watching a home movie, and he was funny about it. He said, "What's goin' on here? Is this some sort of test? Do you do this to all the guys you bring home? I don't know how I'm supposed to react to your high school basketball game." I said, "Sorry, I don't really have anything else to watch." Then he started making fun of the refs, and I was laughing so hard. Then we started to kiss and I got butterflies. I really,

really liked him. We made out for a while, and then I told him I had better go to bed because I had to go to work the next day. We kissed a little more, and then he left.

Look at that fuckin' ref he looks like he is mad at his life choices

Ha Ha Ha Ha Oh my God you are so funny

This was the beginning of a four-year love affair that was passionate, sweet, manipulative, horrible, amazing, exciting, awful, super fucked-up, and very, very special. Fueled by my alcoholism and his control issues, this relationship turned my drinking into a weapon that caused a war. Do I know how to dramatically end a chapter or what?

Chapter Twelve

Right around the same time Vinnie and I started dating, my career was taking off. Okay, it wasn't taking off, but I signed with a manager who wanted to help develop a show with me. I got a decent tape and sent it to the fancy L.A. producer and he liked it I was getting booked for more and more shows. Vinnie was a well-known comic who didn't work the same circuit as I did, but we knew a lot of the same people. He did a lot of shows on the road, and he helped manage an old comedy club I'll call Stitches.

We started spending a lot of time together, right away. He was staying over at my place a few nights a week, and it was great. I was still adjusting to checking in with someone to let them know where I was, but I loved him so much. I was so physically attracted to him I couldn't stand it. I could have sex with him when I was sober and I was like, "This is real love." I wanted to make him happy and was very nervous about upsetting him. I toned down my drinking. I'd leave bars at 1 a.m. instead of 4 a.m. so I could meet up with him. And here's the kicker: Vinnie didn't drink. He said he used to drink, but stopped and didn't really get into the details of why. He simply said, "I don't drink."

A few weeks after we started dating, a girl comic came up to me and said, "You know Vinnie used to own a strip club, right?" I was like, "ARE YOU FUCKING SERIOUS?" When I asked him about it, he was pretty straightforward. "Yep, sure did." Then he went on to tell me about his crazy, former strip-club-owning life that ended horribly. He had scary story after scary story, most of them involving him drinking and being surrounded by horrible people and getting arrested. He made a lot of money, lost a lot of money, and his girlfriend was a stripper, and he drove his car off the road, and people were after him because he owed them money, and got into a lot of trouble, etc. This raised about 900 red flags. But I'm like a bull; I like the color red. I know this analogy is bad, but I'm gonna leave it in here.

So, THAT's why he didn't drink. He smoked pot nonstop and would pop painkillers when he wasn't in pain. But in my eyes, he was pretty sober. I dug a little bit into his shady past, but not too much and I didn't judge him. I thought it was cool how he left that pimpin' lifestyle, quit drinking, and followed his dream of being a stand-up comic. That took a lot of balls, and I admired him for it.

Remember:
Comedy Is Easier
Than Pimpin'

I fell hard for Vinnie, and it scared the shit out of me. I was afraid of getting hurt. I was afraid that I wouldn't be able to focus on comedy. I was afraid of the responsibility of committing to someone. I was so used to being a loner, doing whatever I wanted when I wanted, and he was the type of boyfriend who wanted to know where I was and what I was doing. And if he was upset with my behavior, he'd call me on it. I sort of liked this about him; he never really held back his feelings and was honest and vocal and sensitive and intuitive and was really good at handling my personality. He worked hard at this relationship, and I thought I should start doing that too.

About six months into our relationship, I think he knew I was a drunk. There were a few times I got on his nerves, or flaked out on him, or lied about one thing or another. One night, I told him I was going to stay home, and he could just come over after he was finished with his shows. When he came over, I was drunk; he could smell booze on me. He got so mad, "You lied to me. You said you were going to stay home, and you went out drinking. I'm leaving!" I told him I did stay home, which was the truth, but he didn't believe me. As he was getting ready to walk out the door, I started crying and I said, "I stayed home and got drunk by myself. I think I'm an alcoholic." It was the first time I ever said that. I wasn't sure if I meant it, or what it meant, but I had to say something dramatic so he wouldn't leave. He hugged me and got real sweet and cuddly and from this point forward our manipulative pushing and pulling escalated to the point of insanity.

Not even I can save these people

I think I'm an alcoholic

It's okay come here baby

Life sized Batman Cardboard cut out

Once I verbalized I had a problem, it became like this lingering thing in our relationship—there was me, and there was Vinnie, and there was my drinking problem. I started hiding how much and when and where I drank. It was a living nightmare. The guilt and the shame consumed me, and I managed to turn it into a form of resentment. I wanted to break up with him so I could do whatever the fuck I wanted, but the thought of ruining a relationship because I drank too much felt horrible. Plus, I was in love with him, or maybe it was lust, I didn't know, but I was really scared to lose him. I was depressed all of the time and became obsessed with controlling my drinking and making the relationship work.

This went on for at least a year. Comedy was slowly slipping away from me. I went from riding high from signing with a manager to thinking I wasn't good enough, and I started to sabotage everything. I spent a lot of energy worrying about Vinnie being mad at me. Plus, he was sort of a dick when something good happened to me. If I said, "I got a big audition today. Jack hooked it up for me!" He'd say, "Yeah, well, that's only because he wants to fuck you." Or, he'd say, "I've been doing comedy for nine years. You've been doing it for two. How the fuck did you get into that festival but I didn't?" He was threatened and jealous, but at the same time, he would tell me how talented I was.

I was threatened by his success, too. If he had some heat on a project or if he got booked for a big show, I'd get so scared. I thought if he became famous he'd leave me for a prettier girl or cheat on me with a groupie or something. We fueled each other's insecurities, and it became a game of who could out-manipulate the other. He bought me a bottle of wine one time when our relationship was on the rocks (pun!). Even after all of our fighting about my drinking, he would buy me booze, as long as it served him, or if I was able to convince him that I didn't have a problem. We'd break up and get back together, break up and get back together. Sometimes I was 100 percent ready to let him go, and other times I thought I was going to die without him.

Despite my downward comedy spiral, my managers hooked me up with an animator, Onur, and we produced a couple of animated short films that made it into some film festivals. One of them was called *The Urine Bomber*. My pee-in-the-bag story was now a cartoon. It was so silly. The big fancy L.A. producer loved it and said I should do an animated series and wanted to work with me on pitching a show. It gave me a little bit of hope for my career because my confidence was shot.

Even with the positive boost from this animation project, my mind was consumed by Vinnie, and I was so worried about everything. Obsessive negative thoughts were the only kind of thoughts I had, and I had to either drink or kill myself. I was headed in the opposite direction of the way I wanted to go and could not stop myself. I was getting drunk before I got onstage, and I was sloppy and not having fun. Instead of writing at home, or working on more animation ideas, I was watching TV and smoking pot with Vinnie. My biggest fear came true; I shifted my focus from comedy to a boy.

I discovered that if I made him feel superior to me, he felt better about himself. I didn't know I was doing this at the time, and he didn't "make" me do it but that's what I did. I think he liked it when I was upset so he could fix me, and he could be the hero. I knew when he was manipulating me, and I just let it happen. It was your typical sick codependent relationship, and the resentment I had toward him fueled my desire to drink. He was doing comedy and sleeping until noon. I was working a day job. Sometimes he'd borrow money, and I was like, "HOW THE FUCK DID THIS HAPPEN TO ME? WHERE DID I GO?"

Him: Hey Babe can I borrow 20 Bucks

Me: Shouldn't I be asking you for money I am the one with a drinking problem

Controlling my drinking became a part-time job. My hangovers were a pit of shame and guilt, and I'd sit in them until it was time to drink again. Vinnie and I would break up, then one of us would beg the other to come back. I felt like I was dying when he was mad at me for drinking. I thought about my dad and my grandpa and Uncle Woody and how I was just like them. I'd force myself to stop drinking for a few weeks at a time. I'd just go to work and go home and watch TV. Then, for whatever reason, I'd start drinking again.

Sometimes I liked it when we would break up because then I could go out and get really fucking hammered. I wanted to black out. During one of our breakups, I got cut off at an Irish pub. You know you have a problem when a bartender at an Irish pub in Manhattan cuts you off. I had been there for hours and hours and fell asleep at the bar. I was like, "AH, COME ON. LIKE YOU NEVER FALL ASLEEP WHEN YOU SHOULD BE AWAKE."

I loved being able to drink like I wanted to. I didn't have to hide it. I was free. Even if just days before I was terrified of the way that I drank, I could easily shift into "fuck it" mode and go on a bender. I'd wander the streets and walk from bar to bar by myself. Sometimes I'd try to do comedy, but it was frustrating because I wasn't as good as I used to be. Then I'd have these nights where I would try to find another boyfriend. One who wasn't so controlling. One time I made out with a 60 year-old guy right at the bar in front of everyone. He was a good kisser.

Another time while we were on one of our temporary breakups, I was house-sitting for Jen. She and her boyfriend were out of town, and I had to water her plants. It was great because they lived in the East Village, and there were so many cool bars in that neighborhood. I invited a friend of mine out for drinks. He was a musician and hung around a lot of comics I knew. I had had a crush on him for a while. I brought him back to Jen's and was like, "I am gonna fuck this guy," but I couldn't go through with it because I kept wishing he was Vinnie. We just fooled around, and I blue-balled him on Jen's couch. Vinnie told me he kept calling and calling and couldn't get a hold of me. I felt like telling him to fuck off forever because he kept breaking up with me. IF YOU'RE GOING TO KEEP BREAKING UP WTH ME, DUDE, I'M GOING TO GET BUSY WITH OTHER DUDES.

And let's not forget all my make-out girlfriends. Stacey and I stopped making out because she moved to L.A. But I made out with my friend Lori because she was so funny and smart. We went out drinking one night and ended up back at her place smoochin' like high school sweethearts. I don't like my own vagina, let alone other girl's vaginas, so we mostly just made out. I think she was more mortified because the next time I saw her she was dating a guy she met on JDate, and then they got engaged right away. Maybe she was like, "I AM SO STRAIGHT, I NEED TO MARRY A MAN RIGHT NOW."

One night, I went to a big birthday party and had seven too many drinks. Vinnie was on his way to pick me up. I was sitting next to my lesbian friend Clementine and said, "You're so cute. I want to kiss you." She said, "Do you want to go to the bathroom." I said, "Yes." We went into the bathroom and made out for a few minutes. It was the only bathroom in the bar, and people were banging on the door. Vinnie was calling my cell. We kept kissing, and I touched her boobs a lot. When we finally finished making out, we walked outside and there was a long line for the bathroom. I ran outside and Vinnie was sitting there in his car. "I've been sitting out here for ten minutes." I said, "Sorry, I had to say good-bye to everyone."

Despite the fact that Vinnie and I spent a lot of time fighting and torturing each other, we truly did love one another. We loved in that fucked-up way alcoholics and codependents do. It was so painful and raw. He was sweet and made me laugh. I just don't understand why we continued to torture each other. Maybe we stayed together so long because we were both addicted to the sex. I'm rarely attracted to guys (I wished I was a full-blown lesbian, but I'm not), so when I found a guy I was attracted to it was hard for me to let him go, literally. I think my bi-curious behavior was definitely inspired by alcohol. I loved the mental connection I'd have with women so much, I'd have to kiss them. With guys, I thought most of them were such idiots I didn't want them to touch me. But every once in a while, a guy would come along, one who made me giggle and had a lot of problems, and I could not keep my hands off of him. Vinnie and I had nonstop sex for years, and we did do things for each other that were sweet and kind and thoughtful, but our insecurities and egos poisoned any potential goodness.

I thought about moving home. I was beat. The city had won. I was just a drunk who wasn't good at comedy anymore and worked soulless day jobs and was in love with someone I had grown to hate. I would watch people who seemed to be happy and functional and wondered how they did it. It was like being a human on this planet had become the most baffling thing in the world to me. I desperately wanted to feel better and to be important, but the fog I was in was too thick. No matter which direction I went, I felt like I was in the same spot. I spent a lot of time in the self-help section of Barnes & Noble reading various books on how to be happy, how to live your dreams, how to please a man, how to overcome depression, how to forgive and forget. Tony Robbins didn't work for me anymore. The help I needed was beyond positive thinking.

Self Help Section

Maybe the Dalai Lama can save me

A bright light in my life during this time was the fancy L.A. producer. He had given me a little bit of writing work and was still encouraging me to come up with a show and was always asking me about my animation projects. I was confused as to why he thought I was talented. I wondered if he knew what a loser I was. Liza, remember my boss from Magic: The Gathering and the consulting firm with the cokehead liar boss? She had come back into my life and got me another office job. ANOTHER FUCKING JOB. CAN YOU BELIEVE IT? It was a job where I sat there and did stuff on the computer. It was for a company that made a resource guide for college students in the form of multimedia DVDs. I tried to pretend this was a great place to work because we were helping college students, but I honestly didn't care because I felt like killing myself as I sat at a desk waiting for it to be five o'clock.

One day, while I was at work, Autumn called me, hysterically crying. She said, "Something bad just happened." I thought it was Rochelle. I thought she was in a diabetic coma. Then I thought something bad happened to my mom. I was coming up with all of the bad things that could've just happened, and then she said, "Dad died."

Chapter Thirteen

A maintenance man found him dead on the floor. He was surrounded by whiskey and vodka bottles and pills. We weren't sure if we should call it an overdose or suicide and for some of us it was easier to call it a heart attack. We had no idea what exactly happened, and my family wasn't talking about it. It was like, "Dad died in his apartment and there was booze and pills in there. The end." THEN NO ONE SAID ANYTHING ELSE. I thought about his previous trips to the hospital and how he'd say he just had a panic attack and I wondered if any of them were failed suicide attempts. It was a fine line with him. He had a desperate need to connect but was so tortured by his own mind he had to check out. I went from feeling so heartbroken and sad to being filled with rage, all within the same minute. By the time I made it home, my emotional rage dissipated, and I was just pissed. I was no longer brokenhearted or sad or relieved it was over; I was just really fucking angry.

So sorry to hear about your dad is there anything we can do

Yes there is something you can do - you can Fuck off

"Your dad was here every Sunday. He was seeking help. He was seeking answers," the priest told me and my siblings in a church basement. He wanted to meet with us and let us know that my dad was going to church a lot; he was looking for guidance. I was like, "Did he tell you what his problem was? Did he tell you why he was so mean when we were little and why he was such a mess?" He gave me an "I feel sorry for you, child" look. He knew I was an unforgiving brat, with no compassion or empathy, and he was right.

Being back home felt like a chore, and I didn't want to talk to anyone about anything. Even if I did, who would I talk to? Autumn was a teenager. I should've been the wiser, kinder older sister, but I was a cranky brat and she was pissed off, too. Our energy matched each other's, and we were both like, "What the fuck?" Rochelle was emotional about it. Even though he wasn't her dad, she cried and talked about the times he was nice and joked around with her. She wondered if there was something she could've had done to help him. Adam was taking care of funeral arrangements. He took the lead on this tragedy, and I felt guilty about not helping out. I didn't want to bug him with my feelings and emotions. My mom was busy being tough and practical and coordinating the reception and making sure extended family members were comfortable.

Autumn came up to me and said, "David got wasted and fell off of the balcony of Dad's apartment building and broke his leg." David was our much older half brother from my dad's first marriage. We barely knew him. I saw him occasionally when I was little, but by the time I could form a memory, he was already gone. I saw him a handful of times after my parents got a divorce. He was always nice to me, but I guess he had grown up to be a drunk. He was wobbling around drunk on crutches and told us to come over to his house if we wanted anything of our dad's. He had taken everything out of Dad's apartment and brought it to his house and spread it out on his bed. There wasn't much.

I saw a picture of a girl in lingerie that my dad had taken. I remembered it from the house I grew up in. After my parents got a divorce, my dad tried to be a photographer and turned my childhood bedroom into a sexy-lady-photo-shoot studio, of sorts. He said he was helping models put portfolios together. My Madonna posters were replaced with pictures of women in fancy underwear, and I thought it was so gross, even though they were pretty much the same poster. I just didn't like how my dad told girls he was a photographer, and then they'd take off their clothes and pose in lingerie. I looked at that sexy picture and wondered if it had affected me somehow. I thought maybe that's why I always dressed like a tomboy. I guess, to me, trying to look sexy seemed like the dumbest thing a girl could do because it attracts disgusting men like my dad. I looked around at all of his other crap sprawled out on David's bed, and I didn't want anything that belonged to my dad. Autumn took a little Marilyn Monroe statue, and I don't remember what Adam took.

I thought this girl was sad even though she was smiling and

I thought my dad was a pervert for taking this picture

When he hung this picture up in my room I felt weird about being a girl

The funeral was small and sad. David almost missed it because he was still drunk from the night before. Most of the people there were from my mom's side of the family. My dad didn't have many friends. I was so upset because my mom didn't sit with me, Autumn, and Adam. She sat in the back with Wayne. She looked numb and robotic. I wanted to shake her and tell her to hug us. Her hippie friend Janice, the one who bought us paper towels for Christmas, sat with us and held our hands, telling us how beautiful we were and that my dad loved us. My dad's brother, a doctor who lived in Texas, went up to the podium and said a few general things and then said, "I don't know. He was just a homebody. He didn't get out much." I wanted to sarcastically stand up and cheer and be like, "Beautiful! That was beautiful!"

Right before my dad died, Vinnie and I were contemplating breaking up. But after he passed away, we decided to stay together because I needed him and he didn't want to be the guy who dumps a girl right after her father drank himself to death. Vinnie was incredible during this time. He was at his best when I was at my worst, partly because he wasn't a bad guy and partly because he got to play the hero. He was really nice and was always checking in and asking what he could do. When I got back to New York, I used my father's death as an excuse to drink. If he nagged me about it, I'd be like, "BUT MY FATHER JUST DIED." Up until this point, drinking was still sort of fun. It wasn't safe or smart and there was a lot of darkness there, but I could still squeeze a little bit of fun out of it. But when I chose drinking as my coping mechanism for my father's death, any ounce of joy that alcohol once gave me was no longer available.

I went on a six-month drinking binge that lead me to get blackout drunk almost every night. I don't remember much, but what I do remember is "waking up" also known as "coming to" in random places. One time I woke up on a train in Coney Island. The sun was coming up, and I was the only passenger. I was like, "Holy shit. I've always wanted to come here." Another time I woke up in the middle of a conversation on some guy's couch. He was a comedy friend who I ran into at a bar. I guess I went back to his place but I don't remember going back to his place. It was so weird because when I woke up, I was physically already awake but not mentally. I was fully clothed on his couch, crying and talking about my problems and when I came to I was like, "WHERE AM I?" He said, "Huh? You're in my apartment. You've been here talking to me about your dad for the past hour." I apologized for being such a drunk baby. My blackouts were happening more often than not, and sometimes it would only take a couple of drinks before my mind fell asleep but my body stayed awake.

One night, I stayed home and was researching alcoholism on the Internet. I wanted to figure out if I was for sure an alcoholic. I wanted so badly not to drink that night, but I was crawling out of my skin. I had new roommates by this time. Mike had met a sweet girl named Katherine, and they moved in together. Al moved out too, and I don't remember where he went. A couple had moved in. I liked the girl; she was sweet. But the guy seemed uptight and controlling. He was a bank manager, and I thought he was probably good at his job. He had a bottle of whiskey in the kitchen, and I HAD to pour myself a glass. I hated whiskey. I was a vodka or white wine drinker, but I had to drink something. The voices in my head were saying, "Don't do it. You hate whiskey. You said you weren't going to drink tonight." And I had other voices that said, "Just drink it. You're fine. You're at home, nothing bad will happen. Just have one drink. If you don't, you're going to feel crazy all night." So I drank a glass, then another glass, then I called a suicide hotline.

Google

Am I an alcoholic

About a gazillion results (0.41 seconds)

Yes
drinking.com/....

For Sure
Boozy Bitches.com/...

No Doubt
Get help.com/...

A boy answered. I was crying and I told him that I thought that I had a drinking problem. He said, "Are you drinking right now?" I was really offended he asked that. I lied and said, "No! I'm not drinking right now." I recognized the insanity in this moment. I was crying out for help about my drinking and denying it at the same time. Then I lied to him about how much I drank, saying it was a few times a week and only when I went out with friends, but I was depressed and I thought it was because I drank too much. He said that it sounded like I drank because I had social anxiety and maybe I should get on antidepressants. I was mad at him for downplaying my situation, even though I was the one who explained that my situation wasn't that bad! I hung up frustrated at him and myself.

Another time I called my mom and told her I thought I had a drinking problem. She said, "Well, stop drinking so much." I was so pissed at her for responding like that. No shit Mom, great idea. A week later, she asked how I was doing and said that she was worried about me. I told her I was fine. I said I was probably just drinking a lot because I was upset about dad dying. The insanity of wanting to stop and wanting to ask for help coupled with my denial fueled a type of neurosis that made me feel like I was a prisoner to my own thoughts. I was self-centered, obsessed with trying to drink like a normal person, and not being completely honest with everyone. I felt fucking crazy, like I needed to be admitted to a psych ward. I had a new understanding of homeless people who have conversations with themselves. It was like I had a mild form a schizophrenia. My head was so loud with multiple negative voices that no matter where I was—at work, at a party, lying in bed—I spent the majority of my time trying to outthink my thoughts.

I was secretly seeking information and would read alcoholic memoirs like they were the key to the universe. I read *Dry*, by Augusten Burroughs, who I actually e-mailed and told him about my problems and he responded! He gave me some sober tips, and I didn't take his advice until years later. But I was so excited he e-mailed me back. Thank you, Augusten! I read the late, great

Caroline Knapp's *Drinking: A Love Story*. I connected with her story so much, and I thought she was such a beautiful writer. And I read *A Million Little Pieces* by James Frey which is now labeled as "semifictional" because he exaggerated so much. I just picture Vinnie reading *this* book being like, "YOU LYING PIECE OF SHIT. THAT'S NOT WHAT HAPPENED." Or my mom, who I've never shared the same perspective on any event in the past will probably say, "I never said that." Too bad, people, this is what's in my head. What's that famous quote? "There's three sides to a story, your side, their side, AND THE TRUTH."

Vinnie and I were still playing out our dysfunctional cycles of fighting and making up. As much as I wanted it to end, I wanted it not to end. I had stopped doing comedy, and I got ANOTHER JOB. SORRY ABOUT THESE JOBS. I hated it. I began to realize that it wasn't so much the jobs that were the problem, it was me. No matter what kind of gig I had, whether it was stimulating, or boring, or easy, or interesting, I was miserable. I realized that something was very, very wrong with me, and I was not normal. I thought about how happy I was in high school. How was I so happy back then? What the fuck happened?

This job was at a new production company that was trying to get a few reality TV shows off the ground. I was hired as a writer, which I thought was very cool, but the stuff I had to write was pure shit. We'd brainstorm stupid show ideas, then I'd have to write a one-page synopsis about it. I didn't want any of these shows to ever make it on the air.

A new girl was hired, and her desk was right next to mine. She was from L.A. and said she was soooooo excited to be in New York. She mentioned the bigwig, fancy L.A. producer's name. I said, "You know him? He's my friend!" She said, "Yeah, I used to work for him. How do you know him? Are you one of his sober buddies?" I said in shock, "SOBER buddy?" She told me that he was sober and had a bunch of sober friends. I couldn't believe that that guy didn't drink or do drugs. He was so crazy and cool and weird and wild. I told her that I had met him in an elevator a couple of years ago, and he liked my comedy. I thought for a minute about how he was sober. Did that mean he USED to drink? Or he never drank? I thought about him a lot after that but didn't dare ask him about it.

My drinking had entered a new pattern of going on scary, week-long benders to not drinking at all for a few weeks. I had lost a lot of weight and was barely eating and was looking for an affordable therapist. I went to a free clinic in Brooklyn and met with a counselor-type lady, and she was like, "Okay, girrrl. What's yo problem?" I told her I fought with my boyfriend a lot and drank too much, and she was like, "Hmmmm. Mmmm. Okay. What else?" I could tell she had heard much bigger problems than mine and wasn't going to feel sorry for me, so I cut the conversation short and got out of there. I wanted help, but I just wished there was a way for me to figure it out on my own.

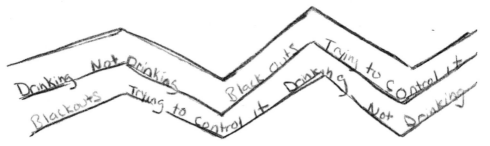

One night, during one of my benders, I drank until six in the morning. The next afternoon, I woke up and had flashbacks of being at a bar with some comedy friends and being the only person dancing. I remember flailing my arms around and people laughing at me, and I remember a friend telling me I had lost so much weight, and I remember being so drunk and drinking more. I remember ordering another drink while a friend helped me stand up at the bar. I couldn't stop. It's like the only choice I had was to have another drink.

What should you do
after you drink 9
alcoholic beverages?

A. Have another one
B. Have two more
C. Have seven more
D. All of the above

The answer is
definitely D

I woke up in a complete state of panic. I was so scared. Nothing bad happened, but I felt so out of control, and deep down knew that I had no control. I decided to go to an AA meeting. I had been to one the year before only so Vinnie wouldn't break up with me. I found it pretty fascinating, but the guy who was speaking said he lost his house and his family and had to go to rehab. I didn't think I was like him at all and thought maybe I wasn't an alcoholic. But after the past year of binging and blackouts, I thought I'd better give it another shot, especially since I drank my weight in vodka the night before. At this meeting, I couldn't really pay attention to what anyone was saying, but I raised my hand and cried and said I never wanted to drink again. A bunch of women gave me their phone numbers, and I knew I wouldn't call them. I didn't go to any more meetings, but I didn't drink for months. I was so raw, aware, and bitchy, but I loved not waking up with a hangover. I was way too scared to drink again but could barely handle any type of situation. I quit the writing job at the production company.

Hey Boss
I quit drinking and
I can't handle this
Crap environment
without booze so
I quit   K Bye

A comedy friend of mine, Danny, got me a job at a hip 24-hour diner in Chelsea, and I went back to my Do Drop roots—waitressing. I liked the physical and social aspect of being a waitress—walking around, carrying plates, and talking to a bunch of different people. This place was constantly busy—it was packed with hipsters, tourists, celebrities, and loyal locals who'd order the same thing every time. I didn't have time to think.

And I loved working with Danny. He was this hilarious, Jewish, gay stand-up comic who I had met a couple years back at a show. He's one of those one in a million type of friends—bizarre, fabulous, ridiculous, and loyal. He brought me so much joy at work.

My favorite thing was when he would fuck with the customers. He'd walk by tables and scream, "Martha? Martha! I told you if you don't take your pills you're gonna have to get out of here!" Then he'd come back by the coffee machine and laugh. There was no Martha! Then he'd go back out and scream, "Delilia! Your eggs are finished!" Then he'd come back to the coffee machine and yell,

"Delilia, better eat those goddamned eggs. I spent hours on them." He just created hilarious, fictional scenarios. It was the first time in a long time that I felt good. I thought maybe not drinking had something to do with my joy too.

Physically I was feeling great, but was terrified of comedy and bars and parties. My life became very small. I worked the morning shift, then would go home, stuff the cash I made from tips in a jar in my closet, and wait until Vinnie got home. We basically lived together at this point. He had an apartment in Brooklyn a couple of miles away, and if I wasn't at his place, he was at mine. I loved the structure and simplicity of it, but after a while I was bored. And I resented him because he was still out there doing shows, and there I was, waiting for him at home. I hated being the obedient girlfriend. I didn't want to drink, but I didn't want to feel what I was feeling.

I did 3 shows tonight -I fuckin' killed

Behind every successful man there is a woman at home resenting him

I didn't have many close friends. Stacey moved to L.A. and took her coolness to the next level. Jen and her boyfriend, Marc, moved to Mauritius, a tiny island in the middle of the Indian Ocean. I was so envious of her adventurous and sophisticated lifestyle, and Marc was a great guy. He was mellow and kind and genuine and didn't control her. I wondered if I would ever find a guy like that.

I'd still see Stu and Andy from time to time; they were such solid friends. They didn't really know about my drinking problem. They knew I was "a party girl," but they didn't know I was starting to hide empty wine bottles in my closet, or how I'd stay in bed for two days because I was too hungover to get up. It's so normal for comics to get drunk at shows, and it was normal for people to be like, "I'm taking a break from drinking." I partied with so many different people it was so easy to fly under the alcoholic radar. The only person who witnessed the insanity up close and personal was Vinnie. Plus, he monitored my behavior like a cop.

One day I was hanging out with Stu and Andy, and they were both so happy and positive. I thought they had smoked some super good weed, but then they told me about a workshop they took. I was like, "Tony Robbins?" Nope. It was something else where you meet for a few hours a week with self-help professionals and you do these exercises and games and assignments where you really break through old traumas and bad behavioral patterns and overall emotional problems. I was DYING to take it. I loved shit like this. I got the info, signed up, and before you knew it I was with a group of strangers working through my issues with these life-coach types. I asked Vinnie to take it with me, but he walked out on the first day. He said it wasn't for him. He didn't need help. In his mind, those motherfuckahs were just a bunch of con artists. Whatever. I loved it.

I learned that my perception of myself was off. I truly thought I was a horrible piece of shit person, but that wasn't true, or at least that's what they told me. And they talked about how you can tap into a flow of life. If you vibrate with the right type of energy, you will be a magnet for good things. When you're depressed and sad and negative, you have a low vibration and will attract bad things. That was my problem! I had a negative vibration and was attracting bad things! This workshop was fascinating, even if it was a scam. I admitted to everyone that I was an alcoholic, still not knowing exactly what that meant, but would get a better idea of it because after all of this work I did on myself, I flew off the wagon.

Whoah

I was going to draw
a horse covered wagon
but this was easier

I want to pause here and let you know that I know that my tale of woe isn't that dramatic. A lot of memoirs include poverty or murder or suckin' dicks behind trash cans, and I just feel like I'm saying, "I drank too much and hated my jobs! BOO HOO." I should've given someone a blow job in a scary alley, or at the very least, tried heroin, because maybe friends and family members would have noticed I had a problem and encouraged me to get help. But I was flying under the alcoholic radar on a very private and painful journey that always led me straight to the bottle.

I am not performing fellatio or doing heroin I am just throwing away garbage

Stacey paid for me to go out to L.A. so I could watch her dog while she went on a big trip, because a plane ticket would be cheaper than a dog sitter. I said, YES. I had been thinking about moving to L.A. for a couple of years. New York was obviously kicking my ass. This would be a great opportunity to check out the comedy scene. When I got there I was enjoying the sunshine and loved eavesdropping on conversations where I'd hear stuff like, "I love your energy today!" and "My agent hasn't returned my e-mails in four months." I wanted to say, "Your vibration might be low, and that's why he's not e-mailing you back, and maybe he or she isn't really your agent." The people seemed nice, but they also seemed like they might stab you if it meant it could benefit them. I didn't care. I wanted to move there and was planning out how to do it.

I had lunch with the bigwig, fancy L.A. producer guy. I told him that I met the girl who told me he was sober. He said something like, "Yeah, had to give it up." And that was it. He didn't really get into it, and I didn't tell him about my drinking problem, because I didn't want him to think I was loser, even though he obviously had his own drinking issues. I wanted him to think I was great and happy and productive, so I just talked about comedy a lot and how I wanted to move to L.A. He said he thought I was funny, and that I should keep writing. We should make a show together, and I should let him know if I move to L.A.

While I was there, a comedy friend of mine was on a book tour, and she had a big party at the Pacific Design Center. I decided to go. I was nervous because I hadn't been to a party since I quit drinking, but since it had been six months, I thought I could handle it. I was feeling good. I showed up and saw a bunch of old comedy friends I hadn't seen in a while, mostly New York comics who had moved to L.A. All of a sudden, a wave of social anxiety hit me, and I was afraid to talk to people. Being around other comics made me so nervous. Plus, the girl who wrote the book seemed so fancy and happy and successful. I felt like such a loser; I was out of the comedy loop and was basically just a waitress. A cater waiter walked up to me with a tray full of champagne glasses and asked if I wanted a glass. Without thinking I said, "Sure."

I had three glasses within an hour. I said good-bye to everyone, drove back to Stacey's place, and drank an entire bottle of wine by myself. I was chain-smoking and drinking and petting the dog, Edith, on the back porch. It was such a relief to be drunk, and at the same time, it felt awful. The relaxed and warm feeling I felt was hard to enjoy because I was also strangled by fear.

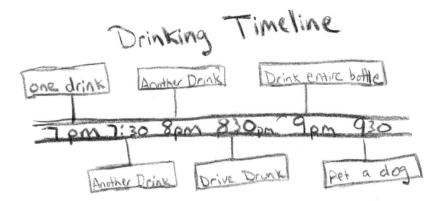

When I got back to New York, I couldn't stop drinking. I tried to hide it from Vinnie, but it was impossible. I was sick of him being mad at me for acting like a lunatic. I just wanted him to accept me the way I was. The only way for me to get out of this relationship and to do whatever the fuck I wanted was to move to L.A., so that's what I was going to do. The sunshine and showbiz was going to save me. I was moving.

My mom and grandma Babe came out to New York to help me pack. I was a mess. I couldn't focus. I was either drunk or hungover, and I was second-guessing my decision to move. I couldn't pack, and I was throwing fits about everything. My mom was like, "Calm down. Just make three piles—one for the stuff you want to throw away, one for the stuff you want to ship home, and one for the stuff that you can take with you." She was always so practical and right. Grandma Babe was scrubbing the kitchen and sweeping the floors. Both of them were clueless about how much I drank. Vinnie and I were still trying to work it out. CAN YOU BELIEVE IT. DYSFUNCTION DIES HARD. I told him he should move to L.A. I forgot that I wanted it to be over! MENTAL ILLNESS ALERT!

I spent some downtime in Pueblo before I made the official move to L.A. I needed a fucking break, and I was really depressed. I thought I was a failure because all I did in New York was mediocre comedy and spent most of my time managing a dysfunctional relationship. I slept a lot and cried a lot. I called Autumn while crying and told her I didn't know what was wrong with me. She was more of a grown-up now, and was easy to talk to. I was just fucking stressed out about everything, even though I didn't have any big problems. The only way I could handle anything was drinking.

I had forgotten about the times in New York when I tried to quit. I forgot about the time I called the suicide hotline and somewhat admitted that I was an alcoholic. I'd think about my uncle Woody and how he drank. He was the alcoholic, not me. He even made a full-length robe out of Crown Royal bags. It was so soft and beautiful. All he needed was a hood on it, and he could be like an alcoholic wizard. I just needed to control my drinking, that was all.

The One The Only
Uncle Woody

I did another show at the Do Drop, and my mom was sort of mad at me because my jokes were real dirty this time. I made another animated short with Onur, and it had a bunch of dicks in it. My mom HATED IT. I was like, "I didn't draw it. I just wrote about the dicks! You should be excited that I have these little cartoons. It's a big deal to have your jokes animated!" I embarrassed her, and I thought she should just get over it. I thought her Catholic upbringing ruined her ability to open up to sexual art. I wanted to scream, "Dicks are okay, mom. I am pretty sure Jesus had one!"

After I bought a Mitsubishi Galant at an auction, with the help of my psuedo dad Hoss, I drove to L.A. Vinnie came out to visit right away. He was thinking of moving out there and came to visit and I sabotaged it. Whatever was left of our relationship, I dropped a bomb right on it, and it was finally over. I could say a gazillion things about what we said and did, but I'll do you a favor and move on. The only thing that was different about this breakup was that it was final. I wish one of us had ended it sooner, so we didn't have to drag it from coast to coast, but as he would say, "It is what it is." I cried for weeks and felt like dying, but thanks to a new environment and "controlled drinking," I was able to manage the breakup.

We are never ever ever getting back together.

Shout out to Taylor Swift

I moved into my comedy friend Erin's apartment in West Hollywood. There was a fat cat there, she explained, "When my old roommate moved out she just left this cat here. His name is Peanut." Erin decided to just adopt him, and I thought that was very sweet. She was super funny and talented, and we explored the L.A. comedy scene together. I felt so much better about everything. I felt free and hopeful and excited about life and the best part was that drinking was fun again. It just clicked for me like it did before it got out of control in New York. I didn't have a boyfriend who was mad at me for drinking, I was in a city full of opportunity. I felt like getting onstage, and I decided that I wasn't an alcoholic. I thought maybe my out-of-control benders were just a rough patch. I was able to experience the euphoria that drinking offered and knew that I had to be in a good place to drink. I just shouldn't drink when I was sad.

My core group of friends became a pack of hilarious lesbians who helped me forget about my depressing life in New York. Erin introduced me to some girls who lived in our building, Lesley and Sara, and they were just as kind as they were insane. I felt lucky to be fast friends with such twisted, gutsy, and hilarious women. We all supported each other's bad ideas, and we spent countless hours drinking and laughing. Erin and I would throw dance parties in our unfurnished apartment, and we refused to furnish it because we needed room to dance. And since we lived in West Hollywood, we'd utilize the club scene and go bar hopping on Santa Monica Boulevard. We'd drink at a fabulous bar, then run across the street to a club and dance as if it was saving our lives. We'd have coffee and smoothies every morning and laugh about the dumb shit we did the night before. All of us drank, which was perfect because it made me feel like I was a normal person who just drank a little bit more than they did. Actually, the truth is I didn't think about it anymore. I was fine.

I had to get a job, and promised myself I wouldn't work in an office because I didn't want to get depressed. One day, Erin and I walked into a thrift store on Santa Monica Boulevard and started talking to the owner. He was an old Jewish man who grew up in Staten Island. His name was Vern. He was a complete nutjob, but I thought he was hilarious. He said he needed some help around the store. I started working for him the next day. When I got there he said, "Do you like mattresses?" I said yes. Then he said, "Do you like Craigslist?" I said, "Uh. Yeah. Love it." He went on to teach me everything he knew about selling mattresses on Craigslist, and I loved every second of it.

Basically, you buy a mattress from a wholesaler, jack up the price, post an ad on Craigslist (it must include delivery, that's what gets people to go for it), you close the deal over the phone, and deliver the mattress. You tell them if they don't like the mattress when you deliver it to them, they don't have to buy it. This way, you don't have to have a storefront, keeping overhead low. I was so good at selling mattresses, I couldn't believe it. I'd sell one, strap it to the top of my Mitsubishi Galant, then deliver it and give Vern a cut of the money.

You know your life has been in the toilet when you end up delivering mattresses and you LOVE IT. My only problem with this mattress stuff was Vern. He was so controlling, and I was like, "I'm selling a lot of mattresses. Leave me alone, Vern. I'm making you money." He was micromanaging me, and I wanted to punch him in the throat! One time, he took me for a drive and said, "Open the glove box." I did and there was a handgun in there. I was freaked out but didn't want him to know. I said, "Nice." He just smiled. Once we were back at the store, I quit. He started yelling at me and I was like, "FUCK YOU. YOU'RE A PSYCHO. GOOD LUCK WITH SELLING ALL OF THIS CRAP." As much as I wanted people to like me, if I got to a point where I was really mad at someone, I would explode and yell and felt great about it.

I am a control freak with a gun

I am a girl who wants to be in a healthier environment and P.S. FUCK YOU

I went on with my life and started to look for another job. Erin and I got along great until I adopted a dog without telling her. I was doing some day-drinking and then I smoked some killer weed and went on Petfinder.com. I saw THE CUTEST husky-boxer mix and just had to have him. I drove to Compton and got him out of some man's garage. I named him J.J. and hid him in my room like a psychopath.

The next day Erin was like, "Why is Peanut shitting everywhere?" I was so hungover. I said, "It's probably because I have a dog in my room." I opened the door and J.J. came running out like a bat out of hell. Needless to say, it was a nightmare. J.J. was so hyper and attacked Peanut all of the time. Erin was annoyed.

I called my mom crying about it, and she said, "Send that dog to me. We'll take care of him." I paid some random dudes 200 bucks to drive him to Colorado and they did! J.J. moved to my mom's farm and had 150 acres to run around. He became my new dad Wayne's best friend, and my mom fed him spaghetti. Happy Drunk Dog Adopting Story! Time to party.

I loved drinking with the lesbians. I think I connected with lesbians more than straight girls because when I was around girly girls I was always like, "Why the fuck are you talking so much about stupid shit." I could not stand hearing a woman obsess about a boy or her clothes or another woman she hated. Not all straight girls are like this, of course, but the real prissy ones, the ones who had rich dads who loved them a lot, the ones who looked me up and down, and I had to be like, "I know my shoes are disgusting and I don't care." I liked lesbians because our conversations were diverse, and we'd talk about the big picture of life and laugh very hard about it. I think lesbians have gained wisdom because they've had to question who they are. Some of them have experienced rejection and judgment and hostility, and I think this forces people to have a stronger sense of self-awareness and humor. I like being around people like this, people who have struggled to find out who they are and have reached a point of self-acceptance through humor and a "fuck you this is who I am" attitude.

All of the dance parties and meaningful conversations made me feel like I did when I drank with my friends in Pueblo before I moved to New York—wild and free and dumb and loving it. I was completely over Vinnie; it took awhile, but I felt strong, like I was my old self again. I was doing stand-up and writing a lot. The comedy scene in L.A. felt a little cold and weird, but I was able to get on some decent shows and made new comedy friends. I met a semifamous pothead comic who sent me flirty messages on MySpace. I felt like my life was a Tom Petty song, like I just had an epiphany, and I was ready to be honest with people about it. I don't know which song, but I am pretty sure he has one that reminds me of my life during this time.

Check All that Apply

☑ I Won't Back Down
☑ Runnin' Down A Dream
☑ American Girl
☑ Free Fallin'
☑ You're So Bad
☑ You Don't Know How It Feels

If you checked 3 or more
your life is like a
Tom Petty Song

Chapter Fifteen

Out of nowhere, that mattress-slinging gun owner Vern started calling and yelling, "Are you selling mattresses on Craigslist? I am seeing mattress ads on Craigslist. You better not steal my idea." I said, "I'm done with the mattress business, Vern." He said, "I'm serious. You don't want to know what I'll do to you if I find out you're selling mattresses!" He continued with these phone calls for weeks. He kept threatening me, and I got so pissed, I was like, "You think I'm selling mattresses? I'm gonna sell fucking mattresses!" I was so mad at him for harassing me. I wanted revenge.

I had been telling Lesley about this crazy mattress stuff, and she said she'd sell mattresses with me. It was decent money and pretty easy to pull off. After finding a wholesaler and researching the market, we discovered that the best place to sell was San Francisco. Lesley had lived there before and knew the neighborhoods. Besides, the L.A. mattress scene was dramatic and oversaturated, and Vern was onto me so we had to get out of town. We closed deals over the phone, rented a 24-foot truck, packed it full of mattresses we bought from this guy named Frank, drove them up to San Francisco, and delivered between 20 to 25 mattresses over a weekend.

Are you going to help me

Big Budget Truck

Yes but first I want to watch you struggle

It was so ridiculous. Lesley did most of the driving. My feet barely reached the pedals in that big-ass truck. We'd pull up to our customer's building, and I'd knock on their door and say, "We're here with your mattress." They'd look at my 110 pound, five-foot-four body frame and say, "Where are the delivery guys?" I'd say, "We're the delivery guys." They'd come out and check out the mattress in the back of the truck to see if it was okay, and it was always okay. Our mattresses were great. Then Lesley and I would carry a king, queen, or full-size double pillow-top up flights of stairs, collect the cash, and get the hell out of there. We were a cash-only business, and we'd say, "We'll e-mail you a receipt" and never did. If someone called and complained about the mattress we would just tell them to flip it over. By the end of the weekend, we'd have thousands of dollars of cash in our pockets and would split the profits and party. We laughed so hard on these trips. Our customers were just as nutty as we were. Hanging out with Lesley reminded of my times with Lisa. Pure fucking ridiculous fun.

We'd get so wasted all of the time, and a few times Lesley and I made out. I was wondering if I was ready to be a full-blown lesbian yet. I liked her a lot, but we were best friends so it was weird. Besides, she had a girlfriend. She had started seeing this crazy girl, Lynette. I didn't like her. She was one of those people who would look deep into your eyes and smile like she was some all-knowing being. Condescending! Lynette was madly in love with Lesley. She was always around and creeped me out.

One night back in L.A., Lesley and I got wasted and went back to my place and started making out. Lynette knew we were in there and broke into my house and started yelling and screaming at us. I was so drunk, I was like, "You two need to get your shit together." As if I didn't know they were dating, and I was just some innocent bystander. Meanwhile, I was a homewrecker! It was really dramatic, bad, and gossipy and not fun. I decided I wasn't going to try to be gay anymore. Lesley and I stopped making out, and I started dating that semifamous pothead man-boy who sent me flirty MySpace messages.

Hello I'm a middle aged man who brags about how much weed I smoke and use my fame to get young girls to sleep with me

← Bong not a dick

Perfect

This guy, let's call him Duh, was so much fun. He was sort of famous, and so funny, and would help me get on shows. He wanted me to be successful and wasn't threatened by me. Plus, he'd fly me all around to fancy events and he drank like me. THANK GOD. I loved drinking like a pig, and it made me so happy to be dating someone who also drank like a pig. He had a really exciting life. I started having sex with him, and then I fell in love with him. It was awful but still fun because he hung out with celebrities.

One time, he took me to Flavor Flav's *Comedy Central Roast,* and we sat with Patton Oswalt, one of my comedy idols and the voice of Remy on *Ratatouille.* He was a Flavor Flav roaster. He went onstage and said awful things about Flav, and it was hilarious. I couldn't believe I was sitting with him. I felt very important, and this made me want to get very drunk. I ran into my fun friend Lizzy and we went outside for some fresh air to smoke a cig and that cancelled out the fresh air. A cater waiter came by with these tiny hamburgers, and we both took one and said, "Thanks!" But we didn't want to eat them, so we just threw them at a wall. We laughed so hard. I loved that night. I wasn't causing a scene, I wasn't beating up homeless people with an umbrella like Joe from New York. I didn't have a robe made out of wine corks. I was just a silly party girl. For now.

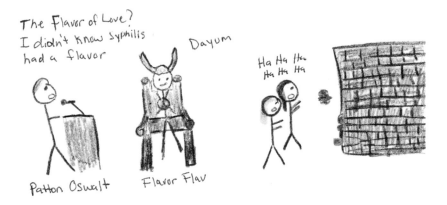

Despite the innocent party perception I had of myself, when my life got tricky, my drinking got drinky. I hope you love that little dumb rhyme. Duh told me he didn't want to be in a committed relationship, but wanted to keep seeing me. I was like, "Um. I hate your guts for being like that, but I will still keep getting drunk and having sex with you." Lesley and I were still selling mattresses, but crazy Lynette hated me. Lesley had to keep her distance from me, or at least act like she didn't like me that much so Lynette wouldn't get jealous. I found myself trying to control my drinking because it quickly got out of hand again. I was blacking out and driving drunk, but I couldn't stop because I was all wound up about Duh, mattresses, and comedy. Good things

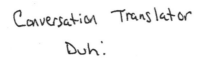

Conversation Translator

Duh:

What was said
I don't want a commitment   →   The Truth
All I want from you is sex

Me:

What was said
Ok that's cool

The Truth
This is not cool

were happening in comedy.

I wrote up a pitch for an animated series and a bigwig, fancy producer liked it and set up a meeting with Comedy Central. I couldn't believe I was going to be pitching a show to Comedy Central. The day before, I told myself I wasn't going to drink because the meeting was in the morning and I didn't want to be hungover. I don't know if I forgot that I didn't want to drink, or if I had to drink, but the night before the meeting, I got fucking wasted. The next morning I couldn't believe it. I could not believe that I specifically wanted to stay sober because this was a big opportunity, and there I was, still slightly drunk from the night before trying to pull it together to pitch the show.

When I got to the Comedy Central offices, I was okay. But instead of thinking about what I was going to say in the meeting, I was obsessing about why I drank, when I REALLY didn't want to. I was pacing and smoking outside the office building, just hating myself. The meeting went fine. I was nervous but luckily there were four development executives in there yapping and trying to make each other laugh. It took the pressure off me to deliver some amazing pitch. We had a few laughs; I nervously told them about the show. My hands were shaking a little bit. A week later they ended up passing on it. I assumed it was either because I didn't do a good job pitching it, or they didn't want a show written by a female. Probably both.

We had another meeting with MTV, which I was prepared for, and they said they wanted to buy the show. I thought, "This is it. This is my big break." That night, after the meeting, I was dog sitting for a friend (not Stacey , another lesbian, Tammy). I was staying at her place, and I noticed two bottles of wine that she had in the liquor cabinet. It was a brand of wine that I knew I couldn't buy just anywhere. I was worried that I wouldn't be able to replace them, but drank them anyway. I got drunk and was texting and calling all of my friends telling them that I sold a show. The next day, I was so hungover and hated myself for drinking that wine, and spent a few hours driving around to different liquor stores trying to find that brand. I finally found it. The brand was called Bitch, and I thought that was sort of edgy and cool.

A week later, MTV changed their mind about the show and passed on it. My fantasy of being rich and famous came crashing down and I started delivering mattresses again, not because I wanted to, but because I had to. It was my only source of income. It wasn't fun anymore. Lesley and I were tired of it, and our friendship hadn't been the same since her girlfriend barged in on us making out. Duh was killing me. He was honest and upfront about not wanting to commit, but he would text and call and invite me out to really fun parties. He even flew me to Amsterdam so I could watch him smoke pot! And he would cuddle me all night long. I hated his confusing guts.

The self-hatred, guilt, shame, and crippling hangovers pushed me to start isolating myself again. Erin moved in with her new girlfriend, Lesley was spending a lot of time with that wide-eyed nutjob Lynette, and Duh was on the road fucking other girls. I was in West Hollywood drinking alone and chain-smoking on my balcony. I hated myself, but after a few glasses of wine, I'd start fantasizing about how great I would be someday.

Around this time a big opportunity popped up for me and I, of course, turned it into a nightmare. A friend of mine was a producer on *Last Comic Standing* and asked me to audition for it. She loved that I sold mattresses for a living and wanted to film me driving around with a mattress on the top of my car. But first, I had to audition to get on the show. I made it past the first round, then I had to do a big show the next night at the Hollywood Improv. I was so nervous and shaky, and I felt like I was having a panic attack. The producers sequestered all of the comics in a room. We weren't allowed to leave, and there wasn't any booze in there. I snuck out to the bar to get drinks. Then Duh showed up, and I texted him to bring me drinks. He did.

I was hiding behind a wall, drinking like a crazy person. Empty glasses surrounded my chair and a comic came up to talk to me and was like, "Are all of those cups yours?" I lied and said they were already there when I sat down. I got really buzzed and did the show. I did jokes about my mom and making out with strangers. I don't think you could tell I was drunk; drunk for me was a state of normalcy. I could talk real fast and look happy. I didn't make it to the next round, but the next day a film crew showed up and filmed me driving around with a mattress on my car. I was really hungover, but I put on lip gloss and mascara and a funky shirt, so I don't think anyone noticed. But this is how I handled big opportunities. Drinking my way through them.

My hangovers had reached a new level of awful and made me borderline suicidal. I'd wake up and lie there in bed and scream, "GOD, PLEASE HELP ME. I DON'T KNOW WHAT IS WRONG. PLEASE HELP ME. SHOW ME WHAT TO DO." I didn't even believe in God, but sometimes I wanted to. Drinking became the most baffling thing on the planet. I didn't want to do it, but I HAD to. I started drinking a beer at noon because my hands were shaking. I knew that I must be an alcoholic, but since I couldn't stop, I just surrendered to the fact that I would just have to live an alcoholic life and die early.

I thought about my dad a lot. I thought about how he died. I drove out to Santa Monica beach and threw his urn in the ocean, and I almost hit a kid on a boogie board in the head. Before I moved to L.A., I dumped half of his ashes in the courtyard in Brooklyn, the same courtyard where my pee bag fell. Now my dad was both on the East Coast and West Coast, just like me. We were sort of the same now.

My relationship with Duh put a magnifying glass on how low my self-esteem was. It made me realize what I was willing to put up with because I had no self-worth. My self-hatred put me in a place where I was begging someone who didn't love me, someone who flat out told me he didn't want a commitment, to love me. All he wanted was sex and a good time. He wasn't that nice, and he was obsessed with himself. There I was, a willing volunteer, putting him on a pedestal, down on my knees begging him to like me. It hit me like a ton of bricks that I was being very unkind to myself. I knew I could do a gazillion times better; I just didn't know how.

Despite my rough patch with Lesley, we managed to stay friends and began hanging out again. I was thankful because I was really fucking depressed, and she always cheered me up. She was one of the funniest and craziest people I knew. One weekend, we went up to San Francisco just for fun. No mattresses! A friend of hers lived in Oakland, so we were going to stay with her. I somehow ended up at the Punch Line Comedy Club. I just wanted to see a show. Lesley said she'd meet me later. I hadn't done much comedy since my panic attack on *Last Comic Standing*, and I was just sitting at the bar watching the show and drinking vodka gimlets. I knew the bartender and he kept giving me free drinks. I kept pounding them back. I was drunk but felt normal. I was thinking about how I didn't do comedy anymore and how I was just a drunk at a bar. I had a couple more then drunkenly drove my car over the Bay Bridge to Oakland to meet Lesley at her friend's apartment.

"I know I have been drinking a lot but I'm fine" – every drunk driver's mantra

I remember thinking as I was driving drunk over the bridge, "I'm fine. This is fucked-up, but I'm fine." If this were a TV show, there'd probably be a flashback of me giving my "Don't Drink and Drive" homecoming speech. I made it to Oakland without killing myself or anyone else. Lesley's friend, Christie, and her husband, Brian, were wine sellers. What are those people called? I forget. Anyways, they had a shit ton of wine and they also had some coke! I drank a bunch of wine and then I was like, "I hate coke." And then snorted a bunch of it.

I was talking to Brian, who I thought was so dumb. I'd always tell Lesley,

"That guy's an idiot." But after drinking that wine and snorting that coke, I thought, "He's brilliant." And this little voice in my head said, "This is what happens when you drink. He's not brilliant, you're just fucked-up." Then they all went to walk the dog. I did some more coke and drank some more wine, and they came back and we were all talking about shit I don't even remember. I just remember we were all trying to prove our points on different topics. I eventually fell asleep on an air mattress in the living room.

When I woke up, I don't know if it was God or the cocaine, but I had an out-of-body experience that was so intense I became fully aware that I had to stop drinking. It was a moment in time where the only thing that existed was the clearest thought that I had ever had in my life, which was, "You have to stop drinking. If you don't, your life is going to be awful."

Chapter Sixteen

It's been over seven years since that moment on the air mattress, and I haven't had a drink since. I love that I sold mattresses for years and the most important moment of my life happened on an air mattress and not a double pillow top. I hope by the time you're reading this I haven't relapsed and am like, "I decided to start drinking again and I'm also doing heroin. Thanks for buying my book about getting sober and funding my new drug problem!" That's how tricky alcoholism is. I could fuck up at any moment. I am not a spokesperson for sobriety, or a medical professional, or an expert on anything. I'm just a girl who admitted I was an alcoholic, asked for help, learned more about alcoholism and addiction, and took suggestions from happy and healthy sober people. The desire to drink has been removed from me, and my life is a gazillion times better.

When I was lying there on that air mattress and I heard that simple "stop drinking and your life will get better" message loud and clear, tears rolled down my face. I thought about my dad and the way he died. I thought about all the times I wanted to kill myself over the years, and completely understood how he just couldn't take it anymore. For the first time in my life, I had empathy for him and understood how he could get that low, that desperate, that fucked-up. I cried so hard for him, and I wanted him to know I was sorry for being such a bitch and that I wasn't gonna die like him.

Lesley and I drove back to L.A. She seemed fine. As much as she partied, we were different. She didn't drink as much as me, and she wasn't emotional on hangovers. I cried a lot and told her I thought something was really wrong with me. She said maybe I just needed a cheeseburger, and we stopped at an In-N-Out Burger. But I needed way more than a cheeseburger. I needed a miracle. The next day, I e-mailed the bigwig, fancy L.A. producer. Here's the e-mail.

Hi, Bigwig, Fancy L.A. Producer—

I'm sitting in a coffee shop in West Hollywood with tears streaming down my face. Gay boys are staring at me. Fuck it. I was in San Fran this past week, and my last night there—I got so shitfaced—I did cocaine. I HATE COCAINE. I've only done it a couple other times, and I hated it. But I did it AGAIN. I can't believe I did it. I cried for a few hours straight yesterday.

The most frustrating part about my "problem" is that I'm so aware of it. And to add insult to injury (that's a weird cliché) is that I KNOW I'm talented, and I'm going to throw it all away if I keep drinking. I'm blacking out almost one out of the three times I drink. It's a massive fucked-up game I'm playing. One night, I'll have two drinks and think I can control it, then I won't drink for three nights and really think I'm okay. But . . . of course, it always ends up really bad.

I'm not sure what I'm going to do. I'm just scared. I'm sorry to involve you in this b/c I know we have this friendship/work relationship. And I want you to know that I really want to make shit happen with my career, and I take it very seriously. I think I just hit my bottom, but I'm not sure how to get up.

I'm going to an AA meeting in forty-five minutes. I leave for Vegas tomorrow to meet my family (great place to go to sober up). But I was hoping when I got back maybe we could go for coffee? I REALLY appreciate everything you've done for me. I know I'm going to be okay. I'm super strong and am actually excited about living a life without drinking. I just feel scared. I have sort of talked to my mom about this, but she gets so worried I can't be honest with her.

Anyway . . . I'm going to run to this meeting. Let me know if you are around next week. I would love to talk to you about everything. Thank you so much. Please don't think I'm a loser. I just don't know who to talk to about this . . . everyone I know drinks. Much love. Hit me back when you can.

Peace, Amber

Within an hour of pressing Send, he called me and so did his sober friend, Sherri. He said I was going to be okay, and he understood exactly how I felt. He told me to talk to Sherri because she was an incredible lady who had a lot of experience helping young women get sober. I called and told her what was happening, and she shared some of her experiences with me. She was so funny and ridiculous. I remember smiling through the tears as she talked about the things she did when she blacked out. She was like, "Oh, sweetie. It got to the point where I would take notes when I drunk dialed people so I'd remember what I said. And then I couldn't even read the notes the next morning! Hahaha!" I loved how she was honest about that, and I loved how she laughed about it.

First Sober Phone Call

I know we have never met but I need help. I keep blacking out and I don't know how to stop drinking

I will help you sweetie I understand - one time I was drunk for 10 years

Desperation fueled my desire to take action in sobriety. With the help of Sherri and the producer, I was quickly surrounded by the right information and the right people. I wanted to learn about alcoholism. I wanted to know what all of these sober people knew. I finally admitted that I couldn't get sober by myself. This is what was different from all the other times I tried to quit drinking—knowing that I couldn't do it on my own and being willing to take suggestions from other people. I learned that alcoholics are wired differently. We have obsessive, loud minds, and when we drink to shut it up, a craving (also known as an allergy) kicks in that is so strong, we have to drink more until we pass out. Uh oh! That first drink leads to many drinks. Both our minds and our bodies are different than "normal" people's.

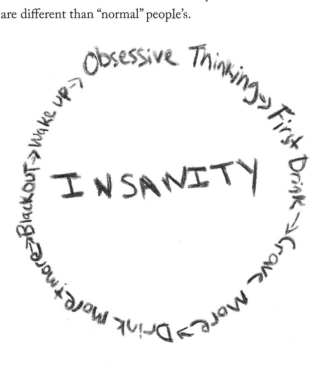

This information was a huge relief, and I stopped hating myself so much. It made me stop feeling so stupid and weak and crazy. It made me understand that I had a fucked-up disease, or disorder, or mental illness, or condition, or a deathly bad habit. I don't give a shit what you call it; it's fucking insane. When I realized my mind was off and needed to be fixed, I wasn't like, "Oh great. Now I can act like a victim." I felt more like, "Holy shit. This is a thing. Alcoholism is a real thing, and it's defined, and there are people who talk about it and are recovering from it. This is amazing." Before this, everything was a blurry mystery, and denial kept me from seeking help. I was so happy to be in this sober universe filled with information and people that guided me toward a solution.

But getting sober was tough. As much as I want to sell you on it and as much as I want anyone who is struggling with booze and drugs to get sober, because it's the most amazing thing in the fucking world, it's not easy. I think if it were easy, more people would do it. Recovery is fucking hard. But if you have a problem, I HOPE YOU DO WHATEVER IT TAKES TO GET SOBER!

Oh poor baby has to feel his feelings and he doesn't like it. Of course sobriety is painful and scary but it is worth every tear that rolls down your fuckin' face. If you want to live a joyous life where you are no longer a slave to a substance that is killing you - you are going to have to work for it So SHUT THE FUCK UP AND WRITE A GRATITUDE LIST

I struggled at first. I couldn't afford rent, and there was no way I was going to go back to selling mattresses. I couldn't carry a king-size double pillow top up seven flights of stairs without having twelve beers afterward. I needed a break from everything. Sherri suggested I move in with her fiancé, Carey, because he had an extra room in his condo downtown. What kind of lady lets a young, shady girl move in with her fiancé? I could not believe how cool she was, and he was sober too and so nice to me. He understood how rough getting sober can be, and let me live with him for real cheap. Thanks, Carey and Sherri, for being my own little private rehab center.

For the first few months, I'd shift from feeling so great, almost high on life to feeling depressed. I was just living out the highs and lows that I was used to. My mind and body were on autopilot, using the fuel from previous years of extreme behaviors and moods. Oh, and I quit smoking too, so I was an overemotional nutjob, a raw nerve walking around experiencing feelings for the first time in a long time—no booze, no smokes, and a lot of fear. I was scared of doing comedy. The thought of walking into a club without drinking, let alone getting onstage, was terrifying. I had never done a comedy show without drinking before getting onstage, and I was like that tiny mouse from the bad cat analogy from chapter five.

Remember me ?

The first show I did after getting off the sauce was a too-cool-for-school show in L.A. I hated these kinds of gigs in L.A. Everyone in the audience is in the entertainment industry, which means, if you're a comic, you're automatically involved in a competition you didn't sign up for. It's a very gross feeling, especially when you're sober. Anyways, I went to the show with my sweet friend Beth, she's real smart and funny. She's won like six Emmys for writing comedy, and she helped me go over my jokes before I got onstage. I talked about how I felt like I had just woken up from a ten-year blackout and didn't even remember what the fuck I had been doing or talking about. I said, "After I got sober one of the first things I said was, I do stand-up comedy? What are my jokes?" Most of my jokes were about not remembering my jokes. It went well and I had fun, but I started to question if I even wanted to do stand-up. I felt like when I was drinking I thought whatever I said was so funny and thought I better say it into a microphone. Now that I was sober, I didn't really care if I was funny. I just wanted to find a way to feel good naturally.

I was raw, confused, and very tired. I slept a lot and I craved sugar. I'd go to a frozen yogurt place, the kind with different flavors and different toppings, fill up a big tub, go home and eat it, read about alcoholism, and go to bed. I was afraid that I was going to turn into a boring person. The fear of not having fun or not being cool kept me drinking for many years. But then I realized I had to change my definition of what I thought "cool" was. Was being hungover and crying all of the time cool? Was begging a guy who didn't love me to love me fun? Was lying to my family who loves me and not spending time with them fuckin' awesome? I really had to untangle the way I thought and rethink certain perceptions. I felt like I was in a school for living life.

Today we are going to learn how to rethink your old ideas

There is nothing cool about getting drunk and blacking out and having sex with disgusting people and waking up and hating yourself

Got it!

Got it   ok   makes sense   Are you sure about this

Sober Students

All the right people and situations started showing up in my life, and all of the wrong people and situations fell away. I found out Duh had been dating another girl FOR AN ENTIRE YEAR and flying her out to shows (the ones that I didn't go to). I assumed he had fooled around on the road, but there was something so disgusting about having a full-blown relationship with another girl for a year that sent me into a fit of rage. I sent him an e-mail calling him a pig and fame whore and made fun of him for caring so much about how many MySpace friends he had. His response was, "I'm sorry. You're prettier than she is." Uh. Yeah. There you go, ladies and gentleman, give it up for Duh. Sending a hateful e-mail wasn't a mature or enlightened thing to do, but it was my first attempt at sticking up for myself. Finding confidence in sobriety is messy and sloppy. If I were still drinking, I'd probably be like, "That's cool. I don't care." Then I'd keep sleeping with him and want to kill myself.

But I had to tap into my rage and be honest. Then I had to admit that I was a willing participant in that dysfunctional relationship, and I chose to stay in it.

Then, the worst part was, becoming aware of the fact that *I* was a selfish pig and a fame whore and cared about how many MySpace friends I had, too. When I drank, I was the female version of him in a way, Duh-ette! The best thing about this entire situation was that I didn't feel like drinking and was motivated to change.

I announced to my family that I was sober, and this was both beautiful and frustrating. Some of them didn't even know I had a problem. A couple of them asked, "So you can't even have one beer?" NO I CAN'T. I was so annoyed. No one in my family has experienced recovery, because if you're one of us, you're either not an alcoholic or you die from it. All they knew about alcoholism is "it's when you drink too much." And even though I hid it from them, and wasn't honest about what was going on, I expected them to understand how difficult it was to not drink, and I expected them to throw me a sober parade. I wanted the red-carpet treatment with a trip to the spa and maybe a new car. I also wanted them to understand alcoholism and recovery. But, nope, everyone just said, "Good for you." And ya know what? That's all they should've done because they aren't fucking mind readers and sobriety experts. Plus, I was sneaky and quiet about it my entire life.

Oh, wait. I'm lying about no one in my family is recovering. Remember David? My half brother who got drunk and fell off of my dad's balcony? Well, he got sober! He took a bus to Texas and spent his last few bucks on beer then went to rehab and got sober. I hadn't talked to him in a long time, but when I called him and told him that I quit drinking he yelled, "Praise the Lord, little sister!" He had been sober for two years and explained to me how he transformed his life. Even though I didn't know him that well growing up, and didn't know him as an adult, our conversation was magical. We connected in a way that made me feel like we were lifelong friends.

I apologized to my mom for being a brat and acting distant. She said she felt bad because she didn't know how bad my drinking really was. I told her there was no way for her to know the truth because I was never honest and I lived so far away. I told Adam I was sorry for not being there to help out with Dad, especially during the funeral. He said it was okay, and he was proud of me. I told Autumn I was sorry for being so mean to her when I was a teenager and for not being the best older sister. She said it was okay, and she loved me. I don't know if I apologized to Rochelle because she was real young. I think I was pretty nice to her, but just in case I was mean, I'll apologize right now. Sorry for everything, Rochelle! I love you! I e-mailed Vinnie and apologized for being a nightmare girlfriend, and he responded telling me he was proud of me and that I was worth loving.

When my uncle Woody heard I was sober he called and told me he wanted to stop drinking. His liver and his throat were all fucked-up because he drank too much. He asked how I did it. I was so nervous. I wanted to say all the right things to help him. I just told him I finally asked for help, and I knew that I couldn't control it. I explained that no matter what my problems were, drinking wouldn't help. I would just have problems caused by alcohol coupled with a constant hangover. We spent a few days together, just me and him, at his cabin in Colorado talking about sobriety and cleaning his cabin and getting it ready for the winter. Then I bought him some books on alcoholism and took him to a twelve-step meeting. He ended up staying sober for six weeks, then started drinking again. A year later he got drunk at the cabin, choked on a piece of steak, and died.

How did you stop drinking kid

I came to an understanding that I can't control it

At Uncle Woody's funeral reception, my grandma Babe, who rarely drank, got drunk. I gave her a ride home with Woody's ashes in the backseat. It was such a beautiful and twisted moment. Dead uncle in the backseat, drunk grandma in the front seat. She kept saying, "Amber, I hope you don't mind that I'm drunk. You know I don't like drinking, and I'm proud of you for getting sober. I hate drinking, and here I am drunk. I hope you don't mind. I'm so proud of you." She was so sweet. Her son had just died. I'm sure her heart was broken, and she was concerned about me. I just wanted to cry tears of joy because I was sober and could drive her home and talk to her. I was happy she was drunk, and I'm sure Uncle Woody would be laughing his ass off at this. I looked over my shoulder to make sure he hadn't fallen off the seat.

Back in L.A., I let the rat pack I partied with know that I was sober, and I apologized if I ever did anything that hurt or annoyed them. They were supportive and wished me well, but one of the things that hurt the worst was when they stopped inviting me to parties. I thought they didn't like me anymore, but they didn't want to be like, "Good luck with not drinking! Want to go to a party with us where all we do is drink?" I think it was a mix of them protecting me and protecting themselves. They didn't want me to be tempted, but they also didn't want to party around a sober person. No one likes drinking a lot when a sober person is around, especially if they might have a problem. Lesley didn't change one bit around me, and I was thankful for that. She'd still get drunk and tell me about all of her party times, and I appreciated and loved that she didn't act weird around me. She'd invite me out for hikes and to the movies and remained one of my closest friends. I loved her so much for that.

I was still doing comedy and was in bars a few times a week. I was amazed how I didn't want to drink. I had a great time watching drunk people. I'm not sure if I was being judgmental, but I felt like I was in the middle of a social experiment. I was fascinated by drunks because for the first time in my life, I wasn't one of them. I liked how confident and loud they were for about a minute, but then I was like, "All right. I gotta go. This person is a false version of themselves." This sounds so self-righteous, but you can't tell me there hasn't been a time when you weren't drinking and you were talking to a drunk person and felt like you were witnessing them go through a personality change right before your eyes. It's uncomfortable. Being sober and aware in drunken environments inspired me to change my environment.

I would leave bars and not feel like I was missing out on anything. When I was drinking, I always thought I was missing out on something if I wasn't out at a party, a show, or a bar. My need to connect fueled my desire to be social, but I couldn't socialize without being drunk. And once I stopped drinking, I realized the only thing I was missing out on was spending money on alcohol and making decisions I would regret. The need to connect was still there, but I was willing to socially experiment without alcohol. Please keep in mind, it's not like I had that one moment of clarity and figured it all out. This entire time I was going to twelve-step meetings and talking to sober people and testing out new coping skills.

Hi I've had 9 drinks and am full of confidence I normally don't have do you want to open up a restaurant or have sex?

Not even if I relapse

I eventually took a break from comedy because I started working with kids with autism and I was exhausted at night. Plus, I needed to step back from obsessing about myself. With comedy I was in a constant state of "Do you think I'm talented? Am I good enough?" I had to do something where I didn't feel like I had to be adored by everyone. I had to find something where I could forget about myself and be of service to others. If you're super cool, this probably sounds gross and cheesy, but self-obsession can be a slow and tricky killer that drags to you a very dark place in your mind and says mean things to you until you feel like dying.

Thankfully, my friend Sonia trained me to be a behaviorist at a school in Manhattan Beach, then she got me some private work with a family who had a nonverbal six-year-old boy with autism who I fell in love with. I'll call him Smooth. He played a crucial role during this time. He took me out of my own head and put me in a place where I had to be useful. (Not that comedy isn't useful. Comedy has saved my life and many other comics' lives, but the way I was approaching it was very needy and unhealthy.)

When I was working with Smooth, I didn't have time to obsess about myself. The time spent with him changed my life. He was this amazing, little kid who couldn't communicate what he was feeling. He had uncontrollable behaviors that he kept repeating. He was like a little alcoholic! I had so much empathy for him, and I felt like we worked on transforming ourselves together. He even started talking a little bit. It was exhausting and emotional and very hard work, but Smooth taught me more about human behavior than anyone I have ever met. I am thankful for that sweet, brave, and brilliant little human warrior.

Sometimes I thought that I had alcoholism licked and that I would never want to drink again. But then something uncomfortable would happen and my mind told me to drink. One time, I was dog sitting for my friend's parents in Encino. They had a tiny, white, fluffy bichon poodle named Latte, who they loved, adored, and cherished. A day after they left for vacation and left me in charge, a coyote attacked him in the backyard. I heard a loud yelp and ran out and saw Latte dangling lifeless from the coyote's mouth. I was like, "Oh my

God! Coyote! Please let him go! PLEASE, PLEASE, PLEASE!" I ran toward them, and the coyote ran away down into a canyon so he could eat Latte in private. I was so mad at that coyote. I stood there in shock, and the first thing I thought was, "I get to drink over this."

Chapter Seventeen

I was going to drink. I walked back into the house toward the liquor cabinet. I was just standing there looking at the booze bottles and thinking that I could just get hammered for days. When the couple got home, I'd be sprawled out on the couch like, "Sorry, but a coyote turned Latte into lunch and ate him," then I'd take a swig out of a vodka bottle and a drag from a cigarette and kill myself. Just as I was finishing up this wonderful fantasy, I heard a *clink clink clank clank* sound. I looked outside and it was Latte, running back toward the house. Everything went in slow motion for a second, his ears flapping, his tongue poking through his huge smile, his dog tags clanking against each other as he ran through a patch of the flowers in the garden. He got away from that fucking coyote! I couldn't believe he escaped. He had shat himself and had a tiny little pierce in his neck but other than that he was fine. The sick part of me was a little bummed that he survived because it would have been nice to have an excuse to drink, but I recognized how twisted that thought was and shifted it to gratitude. I told the couple what had happened, and they were thankful he was alive and gave me an extra hundred bucks for the trouble. A couple weeks later, they put up a fence.

Just kicked that coyote's ass

Oh hi! I'm not gonna drink this just wanted to see how heavy it is

I had one other close relapse call, over a boy. After about four years of sobriety, I was driving home after working with Smooth, and I was upset about a relationship I was in. I had fallen in love with an alcoholic who had no intention of getting sober. Sobriety doesn't make you automatically smart; it teaches you painful lessons until you become less stupid. And I felt like Karma was strangling me to death. I thought about Vinnie and how hard it must have been to date me. I thought about what an unpredictable nightmare I had been. When you're dating an alcoholic, it feels like you're dating three people—the person who is drunk, the person who is hungover, and the person who needs a drink.

I was sooooo in love with this sweet and talented man. He wasn't mean or controlling; he was just three different people. I fully understood why he wanted to drink and knew I wasn't powerful enough to make him stop. I loved him more than anyone I had ever loved, but there was no way it was going to work. It wasn't that he drank. It was that he drank like an alcoholic; there is a huge difference. Normal people who drink "have a couple"; alcoholics have a couple plus nine more. When I recognized this about him, I wanted to lie down on the ground and go to sleep and never wake up. The very dramatic part of me thought about killing myself, but I was always too scared to do that. I thought if I shot myself in the head, I would live through it and be the girl with a chunk of her face missing being like, "I tried to kill myself and missed." I didn't want to lose a chunk of my face, so my next thought was, "I want to drink." I could not handle the way I was feeling and wanted that quick fix, that immediate relief I knew I'd get with a few drinks. I was driving and thought, "Find a liquor store and go home and drink alone and don't tell anyone about it." I scanned the streets for a liquor store; they were everywhere. Almost one on every corner. It's weird how when you start to look for something it shows up.

I knew I was insane, so while I was looking for a liquor store I called Sherri and started crying and said, "I feel like getting drunk." She was at a charity event and went outside so she could talk to me. She made me stay on the phone with her until I got home. I drove past all of the liquor stores while she talked me through it and I made it home. The next morning I was fine. That moment passed and I couldn't believe I was about to throw away four years of sobriety for one moment when I was really uncomfortable and insane. All I did was make a phone call to someone who wouldn't judge me and tell me I was being dramatic and to stop acting like a victim. She was someone who knew exactly how it felt to feel insane and gave me suggestions to get through it.

It's those little decisions in those intense moments that make a huge difference. Of course the common sense thing to do is not drink, but I make choices KNOWING they are a bad idea. I will welcome a bad idea, pour gasoline on it, then laugh as I throw a match. The only reason why I chose to make a phone call instead of drink is because I had been active in sobriety. Making that call wasn't my idea; it was an idea that had been suggested to me and was fresh in my mind. My ideas aren't always that great. My idea was "shoot a chunk of your face off or drink." I was taught new ways of handling my problems, or at least the problems I made up in my head. My go-to solution, alcohol, had to be replaced with positive behaviors. It took a long time for this develop in my brain.

It's a fucking battlefield of thoughts and emotions without booze. I've been really dumb, depressed, angry, and immature over the past seven years. My mind without alcohol is still insane. The longer I stay sober, the more I realize why I drank. I once heard a guy say, "If you want to experience alcoholism, quit drinking." Once I took the alcohol away, I was still stuck with the reason I drank in the first place. I drank because I had obsessive negative thinking, and without alcohol I still have negative thoughts. Alcoholism is such a baffling condition, and I'm sure it's even more confusing to people who aren't addicts. Normal people who say, "Stop drinking and stop using drugs. It's a choice and it's common sense." To you I say, "Ssshhh. You have no idea what you're talking about. Why don't you just enjoy your normal brain and logical reactions to life's troubles while we spin out of control until we find a solution that works for us."

The only thing that made life tolerable was drinking. Once I was hooked, it took years to even know that I had a problem (despite all of the signs), and then when I tried to stop I couldn't. I just could not do it. I would be pouring booze in my mouth saying, "I don't want to be doing this." It's pure fucking insanity. Something had to happen in my mind, something very significant, to shift my thinking. That usually doesn't happen to people until they reach rock bottom. I don't believe people *have* to hit a bottom, but in most cases, it's the only thing that inspires willingness to change. For some people their bottom is losing EVERYTHING. For others, they manage to keep a job and some semblance of a functional life, but they are dying on the inside and hit an emotional bottom that inspires them to change. I always wonder if I had had more information on alcoholism when I was in the phase of trying to control it, if I would have stopped sooner, but looking back I think the way it happened and when it happened was just perfect. I probably wouldn't have stopped drinking no matter what because I wasn't ready yet.

When are you going to stop digging the hole you are in

I don't know - after I reach the bottom I will dig a little more then maybe stop

Almost there

Bottom

If it were simply just a choice to stop because I understood it was bad for me, I think I and millions of other people wouldn't be dragged to the gates of hell because all we had to do was make a common-sense decision. And it ultimately *does* come down to a choice. Everyone who stops drinking and using drugs decides not to, but for reasons medical professionals are still trying to figure out, it takes a lot of damage, pain, wreckage, and heartache for most people to decide. I'm hoping there will be a new trend where people who think they *might* have a problem seek information and help before they ruin their life. Addiction is tricky and confusing and just flat-out fucked-up. Again, I'm no expert. I'm just standing on my soap box for a minute. LET ME HAVE THIS MOMENT, thanks.

I've met thousands of alcoholics and listened to countless stories, and it seems that addiction runs so deep in the minds and souls of addicts that changing their behavior requires a complete rewiring. When drinking became both the cause and solution to all of my problems, I could not function without that solution, even though I knew it caused problems. I now know asking for help and being brutally honest was the key to stopping. I am one of the lucky ones, and I hope I'm spreading some sort of positive message, even though I'm bitching about how hard it is. I just don't want to sugarcoat this shit. Of course, I love sobriety. If I didn't, I would drink because I'm an alcoholic.

Here's why I love sobriety. Instead of believing my mind, I've become aware of my negative and paranoid thoughts and can take action that brings me to a higher plane of thinking, away from drinking and into a wonderful life. When I was drinking, I thought I *was* those loud negative thoughts in my mind. When I'm active in sobriety, I realize those awful voices are separate from who I am. Those thoughts are an egotistic, self-centered illness or condition or disease or a fucked-up way of thinking or learned behavior or whatever. I hate labels because everyone argues what words to use when describing addiction. I don't give a fuck what you call it. It's a very serious "thing" that takes over your mind and needs some type of medicine. Alcohol was the medicine, and it worked wonderfully until it turned into a cyclone of horrible side effects. I had to find a new kind of medicine, and I found the best available, but I have worked my ass to keep it. If I stop taking actions that keep me sober, I could easily start believing the kind of thoughts that lead me back to booze.

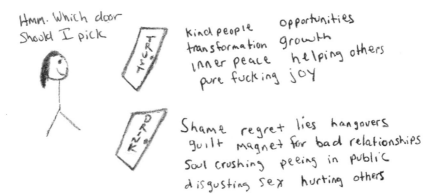

Hmm. Which door should I pick

TRUTH

kind people   opportunities
transformation   growth
inner peace   helping others
pure fucking joy

DRINK

Shame   regret   lies   hangovers
guilt   magnet for bad relationships
Soul crushing   peeing in public
disgusting sex   hurting others

And honestly, it's annoying doing all of this sober shit because, for the most part, I don't feel like drinking. I just want to live my life without having to worry about my fucked-up mind. But the only way I can rewire my mind is by doing cheesy shit every day—writing in a journal, being grateful, praying to a scientific energy that some people call God but I call scientific energy, meditating, being nice to people. GODDAMMIT all of this stuff works, and it bugs the shit out of me. It annoys me because it means I have to try a way that's not my own way. But the work I do in sobriety pays me back way more than drinking ever did. Drinking takes and takes and takes; sobriety gives and gives and gives. The natural joys I found in sobriety are way better than any chemically-induced high, little joys that are authentic and beautiful. There are no more horrific hangovers, no more managing a double life, and I am no longer a slave to something that kills me.

I've just had to feel the burn and work through the low and frustrating times and wait for the payoff. There's always a payoff for this type of work. The long periods of pain and growth that, after the tears, have brought me relief, peace, clarity, and FREEDOM. I am so grateful I didn't give in and drink when I felt uncomfortable or scared because I would have been robbed of the lessons I needed to learn. I'm a completely different person now, I mean—I'm still an asshole, but a smaller asshole. I went from being like a horse's asshole to a rabbit's asshole. And I hope someday I'm not any animal's asshole, and I'm just a good person. I want to keep changing and transforming.

Before   After

Whoah!
That's Big!

Tiny!

Early sobriety made me curious to see what would happen in my life if I trusted that things would work out. I continued to work with kids with autism, and I eventually worked my way back into comedy. I didn't go back to performing as much, but I started writing A LOT. I used to think that I needed to be drunk or stoned to come up with ideas, but without the booze, my mind was fucking crazier, and the ideas were in there. I mostly just posted jokes on Twitter and Facebook and gained a little bit of a following and was like, "Hmph. Maybe I can write." I was so in touch with the pain, I was able to put it into words and then twist it into a joke. I loved it. I used to be so afraid of feeling feelings. But when I'd just allow myself to feel, the way I communicated changed, and so did my writing. I eventually was making a living as a writer, and I finally sold that animated series. It didn't get picked up because the network was afraid to take a chance on a groundbreaking show, but that's okay. Everything has changed for the better, even my passive-aggressiveness.

I have a lot of sober friends who I can tell anything to. All of our conversations feel big and meaningful and real. Sherri, my friend Bridgette, and the bigwig, fancy producer, and many other sweet and brave people are my sober safety net and I love them a lot. Lesley and I are still friends and probably will be forever. Jen lives in Switzerland now. We Skype once a week, and she has read every draft of this book. Thank you, Jen. I occasionally talk to my old bandmates Stu and Andy. Hi, guys! Let's get the band back together or maybe not! Lisa lives with her three kids in Chicago, and we call each other once in a while and laugh so hard about those road trips. Cool Stacey and I talk once in a great while. She is doing really well for herself, and I'll never forget our kisses. Erin is kicking ass in comedy and is still taking care of Peanut.

I am no longer in touch with any of the men I wrote about, but wish them well. I felt guilty writing about my exes, but I heard that if you are worried about hurting people's feelings, then don't write a memoir. I was like fuck that; I'm writing about them.

Romantic relationships are still difficult and confusing to me. I still wish I were a lesbian but am still attracted to men who have more problems than I do. But I am aware, hopeful, and willing. I have a feeling I am going to meet the person I am supposed to grow old with. I'll probably meet them when I'm sixty or seventy, and we'll start cuddling at 4 p.m. and be asleep by 5. I can't wait.

Hello I am an old person
and I finally feel whole
and don't expect someone
else to make me feel
happy do you want
to be my soul mate

uh.
sure.

One of the biggest reasons I got sober, besides not wanting to kill myself, is that I wanted my showbiz dreams to come true. In addition to selling the animated series, I've worked on some very cool projects and had some fancy writing jobs. I still do stand up and storytelling shows once in awhile, but for me, writing is where it's at. I want to sell TV shows and write movies and more books and I want everyone to tell me how I great I am. I still need a lot of outside validation and I have to be careful with this because the joy I get from my career is like a drug. The attention I get makes me feel so good and important, but the happiness is fleeting. The excitement wears off, and there I am, alone with my thoughts again. I'm always self-seeking, and if I don't check myself and focus on others, I turn into such a bitch.

Besides the fun showbizzy work, not being hungover, getting my confidence back, feeling healthy, and not having daily regrets fueled by shame and regret, the best gift I've received in sobriety is reconnecting with my family. Autumn, my little sister, is one of my best friends. We talk almost everyday, and she's hilarious and kind, but if you make her mad she will take you out. She's been the main link that has kept me connected to the family and I love her so much. She got married to an amazing guy named Russ. They had the sweetest and silliest little girl named Zoey, and the love I have for this kid knows no bounds. She's hilarious. One time I asked her, "Zoey, did you poop your pants?" And she said, "Nope. Not yet." Then she looked at me and smiled, like she knew it was funny. I go home to Colorado about once every two months to see my family. I'm present, I'm available, and I WANT to help. I still get grumpy and bitchy, but I know when it's happening and I know how to change it. I'm discovering how great my family is. I know if I was still drinking, I would just show up for the holidays, get drunk, be annoyed, and then leave. I come from an amazing, loving tribe, and I'm lucky to have them in my life. I want back in.

I love my family

Me and little Autumn

Sweet Zoey

Adam has built an incredible life for himself and runs his own technology integration company. (I don't know if I said that right.) It's called Sound Energy.

He has a big house and fancy boat and he lives with his partner, Eric. I thought I was the gay one in the family; nope, it's Adam. I'm so jealous. The thing I love most about my brother is how he loves our family. When my dad was at his worst, Adam was the one who took care of him and I will forever be grateful knowing that my dad had a son who was kind to him all the way until the end.

Rochelle is one of the strongest people I know. She has survived multiple health complications, deadly accidents, and her willingness to grow and change is inspiring. She works at an eye-surgery place as a medical assistant. I don't know exactly what she does there, but I think she dilates people's eyeballs and other fancy and smart things. We talk about boys and how we're attracted to people who we want to save and we wonder why we do that. We have the same sick sense of humor, I can tell her a really dark joke and she will just crack up and follow it up with a punchline. I hope she finds happiness, peace of mind, and someone who is kind to her. I love you, Rochelle.

My mom is still a badass, running both of the Do Drop Inns and taking care of anyone who need helps. She's such a great mom, an amazing friend, and a brilliant businesswoman. She is open-minded and is an advocate for gay rights

Me and Adam

Do Drop Inn Drop

Me and Rochelle

and women's rights. She's real cute and curls her bangs every day and she also dances real silly at wedding receptions.

We still drive each other nuts. I think it's because we are the exact same person stubborn, driven, and independent—but we deal with life in opposite ways. She's practical and finds a solution right away. I'm emotional and confused and make a lot of mistakes before I can figure things out. She has been one of my biggest supporters, and I think she wants to understand me and understand how alcoholism and sobriety works.

When I think about her dad and how he was a raging, abusive alcoholic, I have more empathy for her and understand why she was so tough and wanted us to be tough. She probably had a choice as a kid to be strong and move on or cry and crumble. She chose strength, and I'm very lucky to have such a badass mom.

Oh, and she even gave me her car because my Mitsubishi Galant broke down. I was driving a Vespa around Los Angeles and she didn't want me to die! I finally got that car I wanted. I just had to wait for it.

She and Wayne are still married. He has like nine tractors. He likes to talk about farming and how electricity works, and I don't know what he is saying. He has a real big heart and is good to our family and he takes real good care of J.J. the dog. When I was struggling financially, my computer crashed and he bought me a new one. It's the one I'm using right now. Thank you, Wayne.

My aunts, cousins, and friends of the family aren't just background people to

me now. They're people I love and am getting to know again. David is still sober, and we see each other about once a year. We speak our special sobriety language and laugh about our insane thoughts.

Grandma Babe died unexpectedly in her sleep in the spring of 2015 and as tragic as it was, it was also peaceful and sort of adorable. On her last day of life, she wore the sweater I bought for her fifteen years ago, the one with the teddy bear holding a balloon. She went to my cousin Seth's baseball game and to lunch with the family. When she got home she changed into her pajamas, sat down on her favorite spot on the couch, and got ready to scratch off a lottery ticket. Then she just dozed off and didn't wake up. She still had the quarter in her hand when my aunt Sabrina found her the next morning.

I'm crying right now as I type this, but some of these tears are joyful. I spent a lot of time with her over the past few years because I was sober enough to go home so much. She loved with all of her heart and no matter if you were black, white, Asian, rich, poor, gay straight—she loved you. And, if she didn't like your behavior she'd simply ask, "What in the hell is the matter with you?" I miss her soooooo much, but I'm happy knowing that because of sobriety, I was able to show up on her doorstep every few months to see how she was doing and to have a few laughs. This is priceless. I like to think of her hanging out with Uncle Woody and telling him to stop acting like such a jackass.

I'm almost done, but I want to share one last thing. I wasn't sure if I should include this but maybe it will benefit you somehow. When rage and sadness bubbles to the surface, I don't always know where it comes from, but it usually has something to do with a resentment. My sober friend Bridgette suggested I write a letter to my dad. I thought this was such a cheesy thing to do and was like, "Oh, okay. Great, write a letter to my dead dad, then what, talk to my inner child?" I wrote this letter to my dad in the summer of 2014, telling him why I hated him and why I forgave him. Then I read it out loud to Bridgette, and it changed me forever.

Me and Grandma Babe

Woody

Grandma Babe

All the damn Grandkids

Hi Dad,

I'm writing you this letter to clear any resentment I have toward you and to also apologize for my behavior. I feel like I was full of rage ever since I can remember, rage and fear. You were always in a horrible mood, holed up in your bedroom watching TV.

I remember understanding, or maybe not understanding, but expecting you to not come out of your bedroom. After Autumn was born, and I did a lot of the babysitting at the age of seven, I knew that you could not function, and something was wrong with you. You'd be in the bedroom all night while I put Autumn to sleep. Luckily, I loved feeling like an adult, and I loved taking care of her. Little did I know that it was sort of fucking me up. And when you did come out of your room, you were an asshole. A grumpy asshole who played the victim in every situation. And you were bossy. In my head I thought, "Look at this asshole, not doing anything all day but lying in that bed. Then he has the nerve to come out of his room for five minutes and make everyone miserable."

I. Hated. You.

I feel like this is harsh, but I did. I was ashamed of you and I would be in awe of my friends' fathers. They seemed so nice and normal.

I'll never forget the time you got mad at Adam and me for playing in the alley. I guess for whatever reason you didn't want us out of the yard, which was news to me because we were always up and down the block all over the neighborhood while you were sleeping. And you made us come in, and you hit us with the cutting board. You made us bend over the couch, and you hit us really hard. That was the day I told myself I would never forgive you. I wanted to call the cops. I wanted you to die. Mom said she eventually divorced you because you started to hit us—although I only remember that time and the time you smacked me for calling Adam a bastard, and I didn't even know what "bastard" meant really. I just thought it meant jerk! Every sister calls her brother a jerk! It felt like you were looking at something to be angry at. You were just waiting for us to do something wrong, so you had a reason to be a fucking dick.

I. Hated. You.

When Mom said that you guys were getting a divorce, I pretended to be sad—but I was happy. I was thrilled. I was thrilled when I found out we had to move out and that you were keeping the house. I also thought you were a dick for keeping a three-bedroom house while Mom and us three kids moved into a tiny apartment. I was aware of your selfishness. And this is when your behavior started to confuse me. You started to be kinder to us. We had every other weekend visits and you were nice. I felt like you were doing it so we would like you more than Mom; you wanted us on your side. And I also felt like you were lonely. You had this desperation to you, which I also hated. I hated that you wanted us to like you after you were so mean. I hated going to your house. I dreaded your dumb jokes and desperate attempts to make us happy. I was protective over Autumn. I did everything for her while we stayed at your place. . . . I just didn't trust you, and maybe this is where my controlling behavior started.

I remember you wanting to become a photographer and you posted up pics of girls in lingerie in my old bedroom. I thought you were a perverted pig. Looking back, there was not one thing I liked about you.

When I got older and Mom stopped making us visit you—or maybe the court said we could make our own choice about visiting you or not—I didn't think twice about not visiting you. I was relieved that we didn't HAVE to go. When Autumn went by herself, I was scared for her. Not that you ever abused her, but I just felt bad because she had to spend time with you.

I remember feeling a little sorry for you here and there, but for the most part, I only felt rage and embarrassment. When you would show up at my games, I was embarrassed. You dressed weird; you smelled weird. I didn't invite you so I knew you would just find out my schedule and show up. But I did like the pictures you took; they were great.

Okay . . . now that I said all those horrible things about you, I'll write *about how I'm feeling now. First of all, I had no idea you were an alcoholic until after you died of a pill and booze overdose. And when you died, I was so into my own disease, I was blind to what was really going on with you for all those years. I just thought you were fucked-up and miserable, then slowly killed yourself. For six months after your death, I went on a six-month bender in New York. I went to your funeral, but I did nothing to help with the arrangements; Adam and Mom did everything. And I knew that your life was so miserable. I thought your death might be a blessing. I couldn't imagine you living like that for a long time.*

I didn't know what alcoholism was or how it worked back then. I didn't know that after you became a recluse you were drinking in private. I remember you asking me—when I was living in New York and I came over to visit you— how much I drank. I lied and said two or three times a week, and you told me to "be careful." It was like you knew I drank a lot.

Anyway, for years I was a drunken mess. It was fun and then it stopped being fun. When I did decide to stop drinking, you were on my mind. I could see myself taking the path you did—a slow progression into isolation with an extreme fear of being alive. When I isolate to this day, I think about you not coming out of your bedroom. And now I get it. I have way more of an understanding now of why you were grumpy. You were probably sober when you were in those bad moods—and having three kids to deal with while you're knee-deep in depression and alcoholism—I get it. I still think it's awful and no child should have a father who acted the way you did, but I understand it now.

I regret not having an empathy for you, and I regret being a bitch—even far into my twenties when I'd come home and visit you from NYC—I was a bitch. And I can only imagine the shame you felt when you invited your kids over to your studio apartment. The only things you could offer us were knickknacks you had lying around. I wish I could have taken you to a meeting or listened to you talk without hating every word you said. I just wanted you to be a dad. I just wanted to be a kid who felt protected and loved. I was just clueless about the disease that we both had. Toward the end of your life, you were at the late stage of alcoholism and I was at the beginning. I was starting the deadly cycle that you were about to finish. And I think your way of life and the way you died somehow inspired me to get sober, and that is a gift that saved my life.

So I just want to say I'm so, so sorry for being so mean to you. I never gave you a chance. For years you made an effort, in your own fucked-up way I knew you were doing the best you could, but I wanted you to feel the pain I felt. I wanted you to feel bad for the way you treated me and, again, I was clueless about alcoholism. I'm sorry for everything, and if I could go back and give you a hug and tell you I understand, I would. So I'm hoping wherever you are in the spirit world that you know that I'm sorry. And I hope after writing this letter, I release the rage and shame I have that's embedded in my subconscious and behavioral patterns. I want to seek healthy relationships. So thank you for inspiring me in the weird way you did.

Okay. I love you and I'm sorry.

Love,
Amber

Whoa. I discovered where my rage comes from, and I cannot believe I didn't turn out to be a stripper. I think my dad loved me just enough for me to become a comedian. He was so sick in the head. I didn't know this growing up, but before he slipped into a depression, which was caused by a car accident I was too young to remember, I guess he was real funny and outgoing. My aunt Sabrina always tells me fun stories about how he was before he spiraled into that dark pit of depression in a lonely corner of hell. When I think about him, I like to picture him as this charismatic young man who swept my mom off her feet and that's why I'm here. I'm alive because my dad was pretty cool, and my mom loved him. And I think that's sort of great.

This is my dad holding me

David and Adam and Dad and me

Oh! Remember how I was mad at my mom for not sitting with us at his funeral? Well, I asked her about it and she said, "I didn't think I deserved to sit up front, so I sat in the back." My heart sank, and a wave of empathy poured over me. I realized that she had so much history with him: she fell in love with him when she was a teenager, got married super young, started a restaurant together, had three kids, and when he turned out to be an abusive mess, she left him. After they got a divorce, she thrived while he spiraled out of control into a pit of mental illness and alcoholism. She had so much guilt and sat in back because that's where she thought she deserved to be. It makes me want to hug my mom and tell her she did an amazing job. Check out her restaurant! She has two of them!

This situation reminds me of one last nugget of sobriety goodness that brings me so much relief. I've learned that everyone is going through their own shit and their choices and behavior usually have nothing do with me. My thinking is so self-centered. I tend to think I have influence on others' behaviors, or that their sole purpose in life is to destroy and hurt and bring me down. I now know that I am not the center of someone else's life, and it's such a relief to know that most people aren't thinking about me because they are thinking about themselves. It's the human condition.

I have also learned that I have to wait for things. The quick relief or the quick fix is no longer an option. Maybe what happened with that sweet doggie Latte is a fun metaphor. Whenever I'm freaking out about something and want to drink or do something stupid, if I just sit and don't do anything except believe it will be okay, a white fluffy poodle that I thought was murdered will come running through a garden with a big smile on his face. I don't have a picture of Latte, but here is J.J., straight outta Compton to the farm. Check him out.

My heart goes out to those of you who are struggling with alcohol and drugs. Addiction is a beast that wraps itself around your mind and tricks you into thinking that without it you won't survive, when the opposite is true. Many people recover; many people don't. Again, I'm not an expert or spokesperson for any program. If I fuck up and drink again, it's not because what I do to stay sober isn't working, it's because I stop doing what works.

In my experience, the first thing I had to do was admit that I had a problem, then reach out to sober people and ask for help. Next, I had to educate myself about alcoholism. The information I had been looking for my entire life showed up in the form of AA meetings and the twelve steps. At first, I was reluctant to do this kind of work, but when magical things started happening, I was sold on the process. It transformed my thinking and has brought me freedom, joy, confidence, gratitude, hope, and the willingness to help others.

This way is not for everyone, which is completely understandable. Some people quit cold turkey. Some people seek out alternative programs. Some people experiment with medication and therapy. Some people simply meditate and do yoga and maybe scream at the sun. Whatever path you choose, I hope it works for you because sobriety can make your dreams come true. You just have to do the work and trust that this is true.

Um. Okay. I think I'm done. Oh my God, I'm done. I guess this is where I should say

Thank you for reading this

Acknowledgments

To Peter Steinberg, thank you for finding me on Twitter and telling me to write a book. *Sober Stick Figure* would not exist if it wasn't for your encouragement, creativity, honesty, and kindness. A very special thanks to Jennifer Kasius at Running Press for taking a chance on me and dealing with my grammatical problems with such grace.

To Jen Kirwin, my sweet and funny friend who read every draft of this book, thank you for your time, wisdom, and overall support. To Beth Sherman, Jackie Olson, Jan Elfman, Mark Sayre, Mike Ginn, Tracy Marquez, Jackie Monahan, Leah Tiscione, Dino Stamatopoulos, Sally Brooks, Claire Widman and Fred Stoller thank you for feedback and encouragement, I am lucky to have such sweet and smart people in my life. To Edie Trautwein, Josh Malik, and Josh McDonnell thank you for helping me organize all of those fucking illustrations.

To Sherri and Carey Caruso, Tommy Lynch, and Bridgette B., thank you for pulling me out of hell and showing me a different way of life. You light a candle when I'm in the dark, and I'm so grateful for you. To Melissa Patti, Lesley Roberts, and Sonia Dickson, thank you for being lifelong friends, I am looking forward to laughing with you until we grow old and croak. To Andy Richter, one of my favorite people on Twitter, thanks for being born, you funny son of a bitch. And thanks to all of the fun party friends I mentioned in this book. I had so much fun with you, even though I ended up crying a lot.

And, of course, to my family: Mom, thank you for being cool and supportive, but most of all, thank you for being a strong and independent woman. You set a kick-ass example, and I hope I grow up to be like you. Wayne, thank you for teaching me about electricity and being nice to our family. Adam, Autumn, and Rochelle, thanks for being a huge pain in my ass, it helped build character, and, of course, thanks for being such fun and loving siblings. David, thanks for getting sober and talking to me about it! To Zoey, thanks for being a perfect, little, funny, sweet baby! And to my uncles, aunts, cousins, and extended family members, thank you for making our tribe a fun one. I love you guys. I wish Grandma Babe were still alive. She was so supportive and funny. She'd probably be holding a magnifying glass up to this page, reading it out loud to everyone. Anyway, I should go now. Thank you. Thank you. Thank you.